The European Community
and
Eastern Europe

ERRATA

Back cover, line 12. *For*: nationality, *read*: rationality
Page 57, line 21. *Delete* a) Western
Page 60, Table 5.1 heading. *Insert* '$m' after 'Food-stuffs'
Page 61, line 21. *For*: 66 *read*: 1966, and *For*: 0.4% *read*: 10.4%
Page 63, Table 6.1 heading. *Insert* TRADE *after* WEST

The European Community and Eastern Europe, 1973

EUROPEAN COMMUNITY STUDIES

General Editor
Professor ROY PRYCE
Director, Centre for Contemporary European Studies, University of Sussex.

A series, written and published in collaboration with the Centre for Contemporary European Studies, designed to provide informed reading about the political, economic, and social aspects of the enlarged European Community and its development towards the goal of European Union.

The European Community and
Eastern Europe

Charles Ransom

Rowman and Littlefield
Totowa, New Jersey

FIRST PUBLISHED IN THE UNITED STATES 1973
by Rowman and Littlefield, Totowa, New Jersey

Library of Congress Cataloging in Publication Data

Ransom, Charles, 1911–
 The European community and Eastern Europe.

 (European community studies)
 Bibliography: p.
 1. European Economic Community—Europe, Eastern. I. Title.
HC241.25.E35R35   382'.9142   73–6819
ISBN 0–87471–200–9

Printed in Great Britain by
Redwood Press Limited, Trowbridge, Wiltshire
and bound by Chapel River Press,
Andover, Hants

Series Preface

The enlargement of the European Community in January 1973 by the entry of Britain, Denmark, and Ireland, marked a major turning point in the post-war history of Western Europe. These countries, together with the original six members, are now working together in a group with a total population of over 250 millions. This represents a major advance towards the achievement of the age-old dream of a united Europe, and provides its members with a framework within which they can together shape the destiny of our part of the world.

At the same time the new Community is one of the most important regional groups on the world scene. It has brought together nine of the economically most advanced and powerful countries in the world whose resources are now comparable in many respects to those of the super-powers. In terms of world trade the Community is indeed far more important than either the United States, the Soviet Union, or China. It is therefore potentially a very powerful element on the international scene, whose policies are likely to be of crucial importance in determining the future economic development of the world as a whole, and in particular the prospects for the developing countries.

How the Community develops in the coming years is therefore of central importance not only for Europe itself but for all mankind. At the Paris summit meeting held in October 1972, the leaders of its nine member countries set out an ambitious programme for its future. It was then agreed that its ultimate objective should be the achievement by 1980 of a fully-fledged European Union. Although the exact content of this was not spelled out, it is intended that it should include economic and monetary union, and common policies towards the rest of the world covering not only economic but also political and defence issues.

If these ambitions are realised the coming decade will witness not

v

only a major extension of the scope of the Community's work, but also a radical intensification of its impact both within its member countries and also with regard to the rest of the world. This process is unlikely to be smooth: it is likely that there will be constant stresses as the Community seeks to reconcile the differing interests of its members, and to adjust Western Europe's relations with other parts of the world. But of the importance of this process of integration there can be no doubt, not least for the United Kingdom itself, for whom membership involves a major re-casting of policies and attitudes.

The purpose of this series is to provide authoritative studies of the major aspects of the new Community as it moves towards its goal of European Union. This will involve a complex set of political, economic, and social developments. The series aims to describe and analyse these developments; the problems they pose; and the perspectives they offer. In so doing it seeks to help not only those who are undertaking formal studies of the Community, but also the general public, to deepen their knowledge and understanding of the Community and its implications for Europe and the world.

ROY PRYCE

Contents

Introduction

The purpose of this book is to consider some of the possible effects of the enlargement of the European Economic Community upon relations between Western and Eastern Europe. It is not a general survey of East–West relations in Europe for it barely touches upon the balance of military force and disarmament, in the discussion of which the EEC states will have an important voice, the relations between states in Western Europe which are not members of the EEC and the states of Eastern Europe, or the general relations between the Communist and non-Communist worlds of which intra-European relations are only one part.

Nevertheless, although the scope of the study is limited, many economic and political issues, any one of which merits full-length treatment in itself, remain. The establishment, the operations and the aspirations of the EEC provide a focus of issues upon which East and West have long differed and may well continue to differ. The acts of establishing and enlarging the EEC were based on the assumption that, whatever their consequence for East–West relations, a group of Western Europe's strongest states should form a coherent and permanent association within which the primary loyalty of the states would be to each other. This is not only a particular approach to the internal problems of Western Europe itself but a West European affirmation that the negotiation of a 'better' future for the Continent as a whole must take as its starting point the fact that most of the major Western states have come together in such an association and cannot be detached from it. The East European states hold that they also are associated in a permanent and coherent group from which they are not to be detached and like the Western states they are endeavouring to make their association more durable and effective. One of the most significant features of the 'new' Europe therefore is the 'integration' of most of the major states into one or other of the two groups. Since the two groups have different political, economic and social systems reflecting different ideologies, it is reasonable to ask whether Europe may not be heading towards deeper political and economic division along the lines with which we have been familiar since the Second World War rather than a new order for the Continent as a whole, or whether there are ways of avoiding such a development. This is the central issue of this study.

The quarter of a century which has passed since the war in Europe ended has seen an accumulation in Western and Eastern Europe of institutions serving the ends of the two political economic and social systems, and if the two halves of the Continent are to live together in greater harmony many of the advances will have to be made by securing better working arrangements between the two sets of institutions themselves. The difficulties which beset the path of advance cannot be understood without recalling the manner in which these institutions have grown up and the controversies between East and West to which they have given rise. Hence it is that so much space in this book, which is concerned with looking forward, is taken up with a restrospective survey of what has gone before.

A backward look is not only necessary for an understanding of the situation in which Europe now finds itself and for an appreciation of the weight of intellectual and emotional capital which has been sunk in building the institutions of the two halves of the Continent: it is also the only method at present available by which new trends which may point towards a more co-operative future can be identified. The method of identifying such trends, weighing them against the established modes of conduct and endeavouring to 'extrapolate' them into the future is very far from being scientific; although it can be pursued in the spirit of pure enquiry it must also lean heavily upon personal judgment. Some trends can be expressed quantitatively, others not; some which seem to be enduring may prove to be ephemeral; some that barely attract attention now may in future prove to be unexpectedly strong.

Approaching the problem in this way, what kind of result can be expected from the process? It would be absurd to try to predict *events*. It would be equally rash to take up a determinist position and say that because one set of trends appears to point in a certain direction all others *must* conform to it. The most promising trends at present are to be found in the field of economics. Despite their differences the two systems face similar problems of economic growth, efficiency and welfare; people in Eastern and Western Europe have similar ambitions and hopes for the economic status of themselves and their families; in pursuit of economic objectives governments under the two systems make use of similar ideas and devices, suggesting that strong elements of a common economic rationality are not far beneath the surface; and economic relations between the two halves of the Continent have been improving. In the judgment of the present writer, however, economic determinism is a misleading concept. We cannot read off with any certainty from contemporary economic trends the future shape of political and social relationships. Denied the comforts of a determinist philosophy, therefore, this study rather than attempting to set out, on the basis of the known facts, a predetermined course of development, falls back upon suggesting directions in which *it is reasonable to hope* for the improvement of East—West relations in a period in which the two halves of the Continent are strengthening their sub-regional organisation but at the same time becoming more aware of each other both within a world and European framework and generally anxious to live in peace.

If personal judgment enters into the identification and extrapolation of trends it must be even more evident in identifying what is 'better' or 'worse' in international relations. Crude definitions of better or worse can be arrived at: peace is generally better than war; friendly dialogue is generally better than vituperative dispute. But where deeply held convictions enter into the matter as they do in the contemporary European situation, the distinction between 'better' and 'worse' can become an immensely controversial and intricate issue. To what extent, for example, is it legitimate to compromise in matters of political principle in order to secure harmony or a *modus vivendi* in the short term? Is it 'better' for the two halves of Europe to pursue their own social and political aims aloof from each other, rather than endanger their relations by endeavouring to set up a pan-European system within which doctrinal differences could become of sharper practical effect? The underlying assumption of the present study is that on certain fundamentals, such as the right to individual liberty, there can be no compromise, but that at the same time it is in practice impossible for two systems to exist side by side in one of the world's smallest continents in isolation from each other and that they must find a way of living together. Given the virtual certainty that the two systems will remain in all essentials what they now are during the lifetime of the present generation of Europeans, given also that fundamental differences in political and social belief will persist, East—West relations can only be said to be 'improving' to the extent that the two halves of the continent, in their search for solutions to common political, economic and social problems, find a growing area of common rationality and use it in improved means of communicating with each other on practical issues. It is unlikely that Western Europe would have much to fear from such a development. Without it, policies and negotiations designed to secure a 'new' and 'better' Europe may well prove to be barren.

1 The institutional division of Europe

The emergence of two coherent groups of states, one in Western and the other in Eastern Europe, each with its own political character and institutions, was a phenomenon of the years 1945 to 1960. In the inter-war years five of the states now associated with the USSR, i.e. Bulgaria, Czechoslovakia, Hungary, Poland and Rumania, in the grouping called, according to political taste, the Socialist Commonwealth, the Soviet bloc or simply Eastern Europe, had diverse domestic political systems and international relationships. The sixth, East Germany, formed part of the Third Reich. They had no common institutions specifically their own. Nor, in the interwar years, and especially after the rise of Hitler, could any comprehensive Western European grouping be distinguished. Before 1939 'East–West' relations in Europe consisted of a diversity of relations between single states throughout Europe and the USSR; today they consist of a complex set of relationships between states which are members of two clearly defined groups and between the groups themselves.

How the continent of Europe came to be divided into what are virtually two sub-regions and the allocation of blame for the division are matters on which the Western and Eastern groups profoundly differ. When they were war-time allies the USA, USSR, France and Great Britain were unwilling, or unable, to give much thought to the problem of uniting Europe as a whole in the post-war period. At the end of the war in Europe there were already rifts between the Anglo-Americans and the USSR so deep that the construction of a comity of Europe was hardly negotiable even if the three Allies had held any common ideas about the future of the continent, which in fact they did not. The grand design proposed by Churchill for a Council of Europe with executive powers in which all European states, including the USSR, should participate found no favour with either the Russians or the Americans when it was put forward in 1942 and 1943 and never played a significant part in Allied discussions as the war neared its end. The Americans were more interested in the development of post-war international organisation than in regional organisation and the Russians were already giving their own interpretation of the concept of 'sovereignty' for European states, which was incompatible with the development of pan-European political institutions. Churchill did not, in any case, contemplate the inclusion of Great Britain in his proposed Council.

In the immediate post-war period only one pan-European organisation, the Economic Commission for Europe of the United Nations, was established. The proposal to establish the Commission, made by a sub-committee of the Economic and Social Council of the United Nations in June 1946, was at first rejected by the USSR but finally accepted in December that year at the General Assembly of the United Nations. A strong Russian delegation attended the first session of the ECE in May 1947 and, with the exception of a period in the early 1950s, the USSR has taken a full part in its work ever since, as have the states of Eastern Europe except East Germany. The purpose of the ECE, as set out in its terms of reference, was to 'initiate and participate in measures for facilitating concerted action for the economic reconstruction of Europe, for raising the level of European economic activity and for maintaining and strengthening the economic relations of the European countries both among themselves and with other countries of the world', but it had no effective executive powers and could only make recommendations to member governments: it could take no action in respect of any country without its agreement. In its first year of operation the ECE's role in the reconstruction of Europe was severely restricted by the rejection of Marshall Aid by the USSR and the East European states.

The economic plight of Europe in the winter of 1946–1947 convinced important members of the American Government that without substantial American aid collapse was imminent. When General Marshall, the American Secretary of State returned to Washington in April 1947 from the Four Power Foreign Ministers' Conference in Moscow, where he had suggested general co-operation in the relief of economic distress, he asked the State Department planning staff to prepare a plan of action. During his stay in Moscow he had discussed the question of a recovery plan with Stalin and found his attitude discouraging. Nevertheless, when the aid plan was announced in Marshall's speech of 5 June 1947 it was proposed that it should be a joint one, 'agreed to by a number of, if not all, European nations'. A three-power meeting, to which Molotov the Soviet Foreign Minister was invited, was convened in Paris in June 1947 to plan the recovery programme and

Ernest Bevin, the British Foreign Secretary, welcomed the inclusion of the USSR in the American offer. The Russians, however, refused to take part in the programme on the ground that it would interfere with the sovereignty of the participating national states and shortly afterwards the East European states were instructed by Moscow to reject the plan. In these circumstances it is difficult to see how the ECE could thereafter have undertaken the administration of American aid since in effect it was to apply to Western Europe only and in fact the administration of the programme gave rise to specifically West European organisations. The ECE has continued to play a valuable role especially in research, in the preparation of statistics and as a forum for the exchange of ideas between the states of Western and Eastern Europe. The significance of what it does or can do is determined by the general state of relations between the participating states; if the concept of a pan-European approach to the economic problems of the continent, either as a whole or in particular sectors, were to grow in importance, the unrealised potential of the Commission might yet be utilised.

Post-war reconstruction was undertaken in Western and Eastern Europe within separate institutional structures, both economic and political. In Western Europe the Organisation for European Economic Co-operation (OEEC) was set up to administer the Marshall Aid recovery programme in April 1948; it was transformed into the Organisation for Economic Co-operation and Development (OECD) in 1961. The Brussels Treaty Organisation was established in 1948; enlarged by the admission of Federal Germany and Italy it became the Western European Union (WEU) in 1954. The Council of Europe came into being in 1949, the European Coal and Steel Community (ECSC) in 1952, the European Economic Community (EEC) in 1958 and the European Free Trade Area (EFTA) in 1960. West European states joined the North Atlantic Treaty Organisation (NATO) in 1949. The original European signatories of the North Atlantic Treaty were Belgium, Denmark, France, Iceland, Italy, Luxembourg, the Netherlands, Norway, Portugal and the United Kingdom. Greece and Turkey joined in February 1952, Federal Germany in May 1955.

In Eastern Europe the first organisation to include all the ruling Communist Parties of the regions as well as others (notably the Czechoslovak, French and Italian Parties) which were not in power, was the Communist Information Bureau ('Cominform') set up in November 1947 to maintain a commonly accepted party line. Like the Comintern before it, the Cominform created as many problems as it solved, was abolished by Khruschchev in 1956 and has not been revived. In January 1949 the Council for Mutual Economic Assistance (CMEA or Comecon) was founded by the USSR, Bulgaria, Czechoslovakia, Hungary, Poland and Rumania. Albania was a member from

3

1949 until, as a result of the Sino-Soviet dispute, it withdrew in 1961. East Germany was admitted in September 1950. China became an observer in May 1956, followed by North Korea and North Vietnam in 1957, associations which were brought to an end in 1960 again as a result of the dispute between Moscow and Peking. Outer Mongolia was admitted to full membership in 1962. Yugoslavia's relations with the organisation have undergone a number of changes. Becoming an observer in 1956 after the reconciliation with Khruschchev, Yugoslavia withdrew in 1958 and did not renew its association until 1964, since when it has taken part in many of Comecon's activities at the specialist rather than the political level and obtained a new status in 1972, when Cuba was also admitted. At first designed to embrace all the Socialist world Comecon is, since the Sino-Soviet rift, still very largely a European organisation. In 1955 the Warsaw Treaty Organisation (WTO) (very roughly the Eastern equivalent of NATO) was established, the USSR and the other East European states composing its membership.

By 1960 the political division between Western and Eastern Europe was almost completely 'institutionalised'. On both sides the earliest institutions had come into being in a period of acute political tension between East and West and even when tension lessened somewhat after the death of Stalin in 1953 and the inauguration of the Khruschchev era, which lasted from 1954 to 1964, the momentum which the process of institutionalisation had gained in the dark years from 1945 to 1953 was not lost. Indeed since 1968 the two sets of institutions have shown every sign of becoming more firmly established than before, so that even if political relations between the Western and Eastern states of Europe were to improve out of recognition in the next decade the problem of reconciliation between the divided institutions will remain to be solved.

Any institution of the kind at present extant in the two halves of the divided European continent has purposes and effects which are internal to its sub-region and external, affecting the sub-region's relations with the rest of the world and of course with the other sub-region. Looked at across the divide it is their external purposes or effects which loom largest, and if the general political atmosphere is hostile or suspicious they may be regarded in a very sinister light. The evolution of economic integration in Western Europe has been regarded by the USSR and Eastern Europe as a process directed against the socialist half of the continent, as an 'instrument of the Cold War'; to West Europeans, however, the resolution of the internal problems of their part of the continent appeared to be more important than external issues as a motive for the process of integration, certainly in the earlier years of the post-war period.

As an example of the differing emphasis placed by Western and Eastern Europe upon the internal and external significance of the process of integration we may take the abortive attempt to create a European Defence Community in the early 1950s and the connexion between it and the establishment of the EEC.

In September 1950 when tension between East and West was at its height, the Korean War had already broken out and a third World War seemed only too possible, the American Government, at a meeting of the North Atlantic Council, asked for an immediate decision in favour of German rearmament. In the circumstances of the time of course, 'defence' could only be defence against the Soviet bloc and the fact that the West European states were prepared to take the American proposal seriously, five years after the end of the war with Germany, is an indication of the gravity of the international situation at that time. Even so, the prospect of a rearmed Germany seemed to many West European states, especially France, to menace the future peace and internal stability of Western Europe. Accordingly M. Monnet devised a plan, presented to the French Parliament in October 1950 by M. Pleven, for the creation of a 'European' Army in which national contingents, including those of West Germany, would be integrated at battalion strength under the control of a European Minister of Defence responsible to a European Assembly, thus forming a European Defence Community (EDC). In this plan, there were four important elements: (a) defence against possible armed attack by the Soviet bloc; (b) the containment of a renascent Germany within a multi-national Community; (c) a restraint upon possible American intentions to give Germany too much strength and freedom; and (d) the creation of a supranational West European political community to control the whole complex situation. In 1952 the USSR, which fastened exclusively upon the potential external consequences of the plan, attempted without success to block the progress of negotiations for an EDC by proposing that the four great powers should examine the question of a peace treaty with Germany, a suggestion which in the circumstances of the time appeared absurd to the Western powers. The EDC plan did in fact fail, but its failure had very little to do either with the Soviet attitude or the 'Cold War'. It foundered in 1954 because the French Assembly, for reasons connected with its own relations with other West European states and more particularly because Great Britain stood aloof, refused to ratify it. The USSR, which has ever since sought to give a sinister connotation to the link between the EEC and the abortive EDC project, failed to perceive, or at least to acknowledge, that the nature of the plan was determined largely by internal West European considerations, that it was a brake upon American policy and that it was designed to prevent the emergence of a German national army. Had the USSR been less obsessed by the illusory fear of 'imperialist aggression' it would have seen that this attempt at West European integration had some advantages for itself as a European state.

The same error was made in relation to the establishment of the European Coal and Steel Community in 1952. The plan to pool the resources of the German and French coal and steel industries drawn up by M. Monnet and announced by Mr. Robert Schuman on 9 May 1950 had a double purpose. One was to encourage the movement for unity in Western Europe; the other to bring the growing strength of German industry under some kind of European control. The creation of the European Coal and Steel Community, which now included Belgium, Italy and Luxembourg, in July 1952 was greeted by the USSR as a phenomenon of American preparation for war in Europe. To West Europeans it seemed to have little relevance to the East–West conflict.

It is true of course that both these plans were stages on the road to the foundation of the EEC, that the failure of a political community in its EDC form caused the protagonists of 'the European idea' to turn as a practical alternative towards economic integration in the Coal and Steel Community, and that the EEC is a child of them both. There is a line of succession from the EDC to the EEC, to be found in the search for a system which would provide a guarantee against internecine conflict in Western Europe. But in none of the three organisations was confrontation with Eastern Europe the dominant motive. Had that been the intention their structure would have been different. A 'European Army' containing a fully refashioned German Army might, in the short period at least, have been a far more formidable military force than anything envisaged by the EDC. Had the EEC been designed as a 'Cold War' organisation directed against Eastern Europe, the Treaty of Rome might at least have made adequate provision for it. In practice, the Treaty has proved to be so ill-designed for handling relations with Eastern Europe that it is in this sector of its foreign relations that the EEC is weakest.

Western opinion of the institutions created in Eastern Europe since the end of the war has been less clearly articulated and less clamorously expressed than Eastern opinion of Western institutions, but is perhaps more inclined to see the Eastern process of integration as a method of securing Soviet hegemony over the East European states (in itself an aspect of the 'Cold War') than as a method of resolving internal East European problems. Western comments have also tended to discount the effectiveness of Eastern institutions, especially Comecon, and to emphasise their failures.

The comparative mildness of Western reaction to the development of subregional institutions in Eastern Europe is in large part to be explained by the fact that the most important development in Eastern

Europe since the war was not the creation of these institutions but the establishment in power of Communist regimes between 1945 and 1948 which created a system of government throughout the area based upon common political, economic and social principles. When the takeover of power was complete Communist Parties stood at the head of each Government, sharing certain common objectives and involved in complex 'fraternal' relationships with each other and with the Communist Party of the Soviet Union. No specifically sub-regional organisation in Eastern Europe is to be compared with the inter-Party system for the effect it has produced upon the social and political character of the area. This system has no formal central institutional focus but rests upon bilateral relations between the Parties. As compared with these relationships the formal institutions of Eastern Europe are of secondary importance. In the last resort the Party system can be used to 'integrate' Eastern Europe politically and socially even if formal sub-regional organisations fail.

In Western Europe on the other hand, where the political coloration of governments frequently changes, regional character owes little to party uniformity, although it may be argued that it could not have been what it is without the continuance in power of democratic parties differing in attitudes between, it may be, conservative and radical, but all agreeing on maintaining the principle of freely elected parliaments. A system of 'regional' institutions in Western Europe was something to be generated within a variety of national life-styles and political parties by a combination of private initiative and political persuasion in the parliamentary system of the states. It was something to be added to the existing political system rather than a natural outcome of the political system itself. Specifically regional organisations are in consequence more numerous in Western Europe than they are in Eastern Europe and immensely more important as a means of integrating this part of the continent.

Underlying East–West differences of opinion about the motives and purposes of the sub-regional organisations there is of course a wide divergence in social and political thought and belief. The idea of integration as a form of political organisation or association between nation-states is of considerable antiquity and 'West European' rather than 'East European' in origin. Its protagonists are to be found among the mediaeval Popes, in Dante, Leibnitz, Rousseau and many others who, like such modern prophets of 'Europe' as Monnet, Schuman and Spaak, were concerned in one way or another with the idea of a European society as comprehending, but superior to, the nation-state. Without concerning themselves overmuch with the internal social or political structure of the nation-state itself, they found common ground in believing that the capacity of the state to assert its interests against those of its neighbours by the use of force should be curbed and that a community of states living harmoniously together and devoting at least part of their energies to the common good would provide a more secure, various and stimulating environment for the citizens of the community.

Marxist thinkers necessarily came to consider this conception, when they considered it at all, in the light of their belief in the primacy of social transformation within the state or group of states as a stage on the way to the establishment of a socialist world society. Political association between capitalist states could constitute a reactionary impediment to this historical process. Since the time of Lenin it has been the majority view among Communists that European integration undertaken before the social transformation of the integrating states is in principle to be deplored. This is a philosophical position which antedates not only the post-war conflict in Europe but the Russian Revolution itself, for the year in which Lenin decided to adopt it and thereby give it authority in the Marx-Leninist canon was 1915. His decision has been supported by official Soviet pronouncements down to the present day, through 'cold war' and *détente* alike.

The difference between the social and political ideologies of Western and Eastern Europe has meant that governments in one half of the continent do not confine their criticism of institutions in the other merely to their external effects, but extend it to internal issues. The USSR has constantly criticised Western sub-regional organisations, as they emerged, as phenomena of monopoly capitalism damaging to the political and economic interests of Western European workers; it is a widespread view in Western Europe that East European sub-regional institutions are designed to strengthen Soviet control of the non-Russian states and to stifle the emergence of individual freedom. These are attitudes of mind which are likely to persist for as long as men and women hold strong and opposed views of the purposes of political and social organisation. Criticism of the internal affairs of a nation state by nationals of other states is still deeply resented by most states in Europe, whether the criticism comes from within the sub-region or from outside it, as a form of 'interference'. Acceptance of the right to hold and express divergent views about any European issue regardless of frontiers will be one of the marks of the emergence of a rational European comity, from which those states which deny the right of free speech must inevitably exclude themselves. How this intellectual revolution is to be accomplished is by no means clear.

One minor step forward might be made by banishing the expression 'the Cold War' from the discussion of contemporary problems. It was devised in 1947 by Walter Lippmann, the American political writer, to describe the situation of two alliances manoeuvring in the dark, believing the worst of each other's intentions, unable to find a common language in which to communicate, always in fear that political operations might suddenly turn into armed aggression and on the verge of finding their worst fears realised, as in the period of the Korean War (1950–1953). This state of affairs has changed in innumerable ways, yet it is virtually impossible to fix a date on which the 'Cold War' ended —or even when it began. Historians differ by as much as thirty years in dating its beginning: some will go back to the Russian Revolution in 1917, others to the Potsdam Conference of 1945, others again to 1946 or 1947. Nor can any precise date be given for its end. One possibility is that the adoption of the doctrine of co-existence by the USSR in the mid-fifties is the turning point, but this still leaves us to account for the nature of the Berlin crises between 1958 and 1961, the Cuba crisis of 1962, the Czechoslovak events of 1968 and the Vietnam War. Some would say that it was brought to an end by the nuclear stalemate in the 1960s, others that in a very real sense it has in fact not ended since the contest between the Communist and non-Communist powers to extend their spheres of influence by means short of armed conflict has not ceased, the Marx-Leninist ideology is no more reconcilable with the political doctrines of liberalism now than it was twenty, fifty or even a hundred years ago, and fear of subversion has not been finally dispelled, and no state—least of all the USSR—behaves as if it had.

On the other hand although these are serious considerations, there is a difference in the political 'atmosphere' of Europe as between, say 1952 and 1972. For any politically conscious person who has lived through the period the difference is unmistakable, if difficult to define. Under the 'umbrella' of the bi-polar balance of nuclear forces tempers have cooled, provocative actions have become fewer, issues like the 'German problem' of the 1940s and 1950s have lost their explosive quality and there is a more widespread belief on both sides that the other is at least seeking for a *modus vivendi*. This progress has not been achieved by victory or defeat in a definable historical event called the Cold War. Nor on the other hand have many of the positions on fundamental issues held by the two sides during the period of greatest tension been abandoned.

Used in relation to the development of regional integration in Western and Eastern Europe the expression creates confusion. To the extent that there was a phase of European history legitimately called the 'Cold War', all states and their citizens on both sides were caught up in it: if the 'Cold War' has ended no organisation on either side can any longer be its instrument. Imprecise and confusing though it is the term is still used pejoratively when East and West differ about the purposes and effects of the institutions they have created.

Western and Eastern Europe have, in fact, different institutional

9

structures deriving in part from different social and political doctrines, in part from a particular political situation in the aftermath of the Second World War, and argument about their 'Cold War' character is irrelevant and misleading. The problem is whether the two systems will remain aloof, whether they will find means of living together 'bilaterally' in their present form, whether they will develop some kind of pan-European super-structure which, while leaving their basic differences undisturbed, will add specifically all-European institutions to the existing structures or, lastly, whether by modifying their traditional conduct they will develop a one-European form of society of which, in a real sense, all Europeans will be citizens.

None of the events in the field of East–West relations in recent years has given a clear pointer to the direction in which a long-term solution will be found. The USSR and Germany have concluded a treaty which renounces the use of force but clearly recognises the Western affiliation of the Federal Republic, a treaty on Berlin has removed some of the causes of tension which have arisen over the status of that city; a dialogue between Western and Eastern Germany has begun, a European Security Conference is in the offing and on both the Western and Eastern sides the expressed intention is towards *détente*. The USSR sponsors, in very general terms, the idea of pan-European security and co-operation. All these are indications of an 'atmosphere' rather than of fundamental change in the long-term relationships between the systems of institutions and of the ideas which underlie them. The enlargement of the EEC and the closer integration of Comecon, which at first sight seems to represent a sharpening of the division between the two sets of institutions rather than their reconciliation, will subject this 'atmosphere' to a severe test in the next decade.

2 Economic integration in Western and Eastern Europe

Both the enlarged EEC to which the major industrial nations of Western Europe will belong, and Comecon, to which all the Communist states of Eastern Europe except Albania and Yugoslavia (which has a form of association) belong, proclaim as a general aim the furtherance of the economic welfare of the citizens of the member-states. Article 2 of the Treaty of Rome sets out the aim of the EEC as being to 'promote throughout the Community a harmonious development of economic activites, a continuous and balanced expansion, an increased stability, an accelerated raising of the standard of living and close relations between its member-states'. Article 1 of the Comecon statutes of 1960 expresses the same general aspiration: 'The purpose of the Council for Mutual Economic Assistance is to promote, by uniting and co-ordinating the efforts of the member-countries of the Council, the planned development of the national economy, the acceleration of economic and technical progress in these countries, the raising of the level of industrialisation in the industrially less-developed countries, a steady increase in the productivity of labour and a constant improvement in the welfare of the peoples of the member-countries of the Council'.

The Treaty of Rome, although it speaks of an 'ever closer union among the European peoples', makes no specific statements about the political relationships between its member-states or their internal or external political orientation comparable with those made in a major document issued by Comecon on 7 August 1971 which represents the outcome of three years' discussion between its member-states. This document, entitled 'Comprehensive Programme for the further intensification and improvement of co-operation between the member-countries of the Council for Mutual Economic Assistance and for the development of their socialist economic integration' (referred to as 'the

Comecon programme' in this book), makes the political assumptions, upon which Comecon integration rests, very clear: 'Co-operation between socialist countries is based on the foundation which has been laid in each country (public ownership of the means of production), on a uniform state structure (the power of the people with the working class at its head) and on a single ideology, that of Marx–Leninism'. Of internal political relationships, the programme says: 'Socialist integration is conducted on a purely voluntary basis, is not accompanied by the creation of any supranational organs and does not affect internal planning problems or the financial and accounting activities of organisations'. Of the external aims of Comecon, the programme says: 'The further intensification and improvement of co-operation and the development of socialist economic integration promote the growth of the economic power of the world socialist system, strengthen the economies of the individual countries and constitute an important factor in the consolidation of the socialist system's unity and its supremacy over capitalism in all spheres of public life and in ensuring victory in the contest between socialism and capitalism'. Finally, 'the strengthening of the defence potential of the Comecon member-countries' is given as one of the aims of integration.

The contrast between the political assumptions and explicit political aims of the two organisations is striking. Whereas in Western Europe the political orientation of the EEC as a whole or its member-states is left as an open question (any government may swing between 'right' and 'left' or the majority of governments might follow such a pattern), the political basis of Comecon is fixed; the Communist system established since the war is manifestly seen as unchangeable. Whereas the Treaty of Rome does not explicitly commit the member-states to any general principle governing their political relationships one with another, Comecon specifically rejects—at least in principle—the concept of supranationalism, evidently on the assumption that the uniformity of the political system should render it unnecessary. Whereas the Treaty of Rome sets out no political world-role for the EEC the programme of Comecon establishes the aims of 'growing economic power' and 'victory' in the contest between 'socialism and capitalism'. In Western Europe economic integration precedes political integration: in Eastern Europe political unity is assumed to be the foundation upon which economic integration is to be built.

Superficially it would seem that the uniformity of the political system in Eastern Europe, under which every country is governed by a Communist Party loyal to a common ideology, speaking the same political language to its neighbours, sharing the same objectives and maintaining close relations within a Marxist fraternity, should confer an immense advantage when measures of economic integration are under discussion. Yet by any strict definition of the term 'integration' Comecon has lagged behind the EEC since 1958.

Professor Wiles, in his book *Communist International Economics*, holds that two countries can be said to be fully integrated if they are subject without artificial distinction or barrier to one market or one planner. To be 'integrated' in this sense their economies must be assimilated, e.g. the same real incomes must be paid to people doing the same work in both countries and tax structures must be the same. There may be some merit, while continuing to accept the 'assimilation' requirement, in adding an extension to Professor Wiles's definition and say that integration has also occurred between two countries when they are subject without artificial distinction or barrier to the *same combination* of plan and market, since in the modern world there are few 'pure' markets or 'pure' planned economies.

The EEC has made considerable progress towards the establishment of 'one market' in the past decade and a half but Eastern Europe has moved only slightly towards subjection to 'one planner'. The reasons for this difference are threefold: (*a*) while a single integrated market was a primary objective of the EEC from the outset the concept of 'integration' itself is comparatively new in Comecon; (*b*) while the EEC states have a reasonably clear conception of what an integrated market should look like, the East European states have in the past decade been reconsidering the nature of planning and are still not unanimous about it; (*c*) it is inherently more difficult to integrate the national plans of several countries—even if they are eager to do so —than it is to integrate market economies.

The Treaty of Rome itself provides for the establishment of a customs union within which the free movement of labour and capital is to be assured, and common rules of competition, harmonisation of taxation and a common agricultural market; laws are to be harmonised, economic policies co-ordinated and a common external commercial policy established. Community institutions are created to put these measures into effect and to establish policies for the Community as a whole. The Treaty is a model for integration which, while never using the expression supranationalism, implies it at every turn. It was not until 1968 that the states of Comecon began to make regular use of the term 'integration' and even now, as will be seen from the full title of the comprehensive programme, the word is still used in double harness with 'co-operation' which is the underlying concept of the Comecon statutes of 1960.

Until 1956 Comecon was largely inactive. Its Council met only once between 1949 and the spring of 1954. After the death of Stalin, and challenged by the launching of the integration movement in Western Europe, the organisation came to life. Its institutional structure began to be strengthened in 1956. In 1962, and again challenged by the rapid progress of the EEC and by a recession in their own economies, the Party leaders carried out a searching examination of the system, and Khruschchev came forward with a hastily prepared proposal for a central planning organisation which would in effect have imposed specialisation between the states by authoritarian direction. Khruschchev's scheme was opposed most openly by the Rumanians, who sensed that it would impede their own national industrialisation plans, but it lacked any consistent champion among the other Comecon states in the years that followed.

The dispute about central planning coincided in point of time with a movement for economic reform in all the East European states, begun in 1963 in East Germany and followed in Poland and the USSR in 1965, Czechoslovakia in 1966, Rumania in 1967 and finally Hungary in 1968. The basis of the reform was a certain devolution of responsibility in the planning process to industrial associations and enterprises, a reduction in the number of largely quantitative planning directives from the central economic authorities, limited adoption of methods of 'managing' the economy by the use of the control of credit and experiments in the use of prices and wage-differentials to adjust supply and demand and stimulate initiative. Not only were these measures adopted at different times by the member-states but when putting them into practice each state tended to apply elements of the reform to its own national system in a different way. In consequence, the national systems began to diverge, greatly increasing the difficulty of co-ordinating them in an international socialist system.

Even before the invasion of Czechoslovakia in August 1968, the Comecon states were preparing for a further and more fundamental reappraisal of the organisation's purpose and methods. It was in 1968 that the term 'integration' first began to be commonly used. Mr Brezhnev used it at the 5th Congress of the Polish Communist Party in November of that year. There was a lively public discussion of Comecon reform, to which economic experts and senior party officials in all the East European states contributed, the central issue being the reconciliation of the new methods of economic management adopted by the national states with the requirements of a more closely 'integrated' community; how to add community institutions and methods to the existing ones without running headlong into political troubles over sovereignty. In April 1969 an extraordinary session of the Comecon Council was held at which agreement upon longer-term action was reached, but it was not until a major special meeting of the Council in May 1970 that the outline of the new system began to appear, an amalgam of ideas derived from the discussion from which the most advanced reforming ideas had been excluded but at the same time allowing only limited concessions to the centralisers. Finally in July 1971, at the 25th meeting of the Council held in Bucharest, the comprehensive programme of development extending over 15–20 years was adopted, in which the concept of integration finds a place.

A thorough comparison of the EEC and Comecon methods of integration is beyond the scope of the present study, but it is necessary for an understanding of East–West economic relations in Europe to attempt a brief one, in particular to demonstrate that the two systems are differently endowed with means and powers. The market economies of the Six had at their disposal, and made full use of, an economic device which could at one dramatic stroke bring a high degree of integration into one market. This was the customs union, which abolished all tariffs between the Six countries and amalgamated external tariffs into one. The creation of the customs union between 1959 and 1968 produced or was associated with a dramatic rise in EEC intra-trade and growth rates. The effect was so strong and so striking that not even serious differences on other issues between the Six could lead to its dismantling. The Comecon countries, since they are not market economies, have no such device at their disposal. Their intra-trade has been managed by a system of bilateral agreements which have hitherto fixed, very largely in quantitative terms, the flow of commodities between one member-state and another. Since there are no tariffs the theatrical effect of creating a customs union is denied them: there is nothing they can do to produce integration at one stroke, short of adopting a single plan for the whole area, a solution bristling with political difficulties. The 1971 Comecon programme makes it clear that intra-trade will continue to be governed by trade agreements between the member-states: 'To ensure their stable economic development, the CMEA countries will continue to conclude long-term trade agreements and also the annual protocols concerning reciprocal deliveries of goods which form the basis for the development of the exchange of goods between them. . . . Such agreements are a tried and tested way of providing the economy, on a planned basis, with the necessary machinery, raw materials, basic supplies and other goods . . . and also of ensuring that the goods supplied are sold.' This system has in the past ensured that the Comecon states transact a large part of their trade with each other and that the commodity exchanges between them are reasonably stable, but since the agreements are related to domestic plans and the central institutions of Comecon are also involved in drawing them up, the process of establishing the pattern of trade is laborious. It seems to take about three years of preparation and bargaining to establish the pattern in relation to the national five-year plans, the result is comparatively inflexible, and because to a large extent trade must still balance between pairs of trading partners some commodities must be included for the sake of balancing rather than for the satisfaction of particular demands.

Within the customs union the Treaty of Rome envisages the development of most of the characteristics of a single market, full mobility of labour between one state and another—free movement of capital and freedom to establish services. Neither the 1960 statutes nor the 1971 programme of Comecon envisages integration of this kind. There is in fact very little mobility of labour between one state and another; there is no free movement of investment capital since 'capital' is the property of the individual states. It is because 'factors of production' are largely immobile that the Comecon states have had to use formal 'specialisation agreements' in an attempt to reproduce the economics of scale and location which in a market economy arise from factor mobility.

Both organisations are deeply concerned with the scale of production within their boundaries. Here, even within the EEC, some state and Community intervention in the 'free play of the market' is envisaged. The Commission published a memorandum on industrial policy (the 'Colonna Memorandum') in March 1970 which was discussed by the Council of Ministers in June. Among the ten matters of particular concern listed by the Council were the development of an effective common market in certain technological sectors, the facilitation of transnational industrial regrouping within the Community and legal aspects of co-operation between enterprises. These discussions are still in progress and industrial policy is as yet in its infancy in the EEC. The Comecon programme is concerned with the same issues: 'The Comecon countries will engage in . . . the joint planning of individual branches of industry and types of production with a view to achieving outstanding scientific and technical results. . . .' 'The Comecon countries will map out . . . measures to improve the work of both existing and newly created international organisations. The main function of inter-state organisations is to co-ordinate the activities of the participating countries as regards co-operation and collaboration in particular economic, scientific and technical fields, in particular sectors and sub-sectors and in respect of particular types of products.' 'The principal functions of international industrial combines (or organisations) are co-ordination of the work of participating organisations as regards co-operation and collaboration, joint industrial activity in particular sectors of production, technological development, foreign trade and so on.'

The Colonna Memorandum speaks chiefly of removing obstacles and providing encouragement: the Comecon programme insists that the international organisations shall not have supranational authority but relate their work to that of the national planning authorities, an infinitely more complex notion.

However, in this sphere there is a good deal of common ground.

Comecon has no plans for an agricultural common market comparable with that of the EEC but is to concentrate upon the co-ordination of long-term plans in respect of agreed types of products and branches of production, specialisation in production and increased reciprocal deliveries of goods and services. A very large part of the programme is devoted to detailed plans for the development of particular industrial sectors. For energy there is to be 'the conceptual structure' of fuel and power balances for 1980. The EEC has been endeavouring to establish a common energy policy since 1959. Detailed plans are laid down for iron and steel, non-ferrous metals, mechanical engineering, radio and electronics, chemicals and light industry. In all these spheres the distinctive concern of a planning system with *production* is evident as against the concern of the EEC for the market.

The role of 'planning' within the EEC is as yet unclear. In a sense all the proposals for measures of integration require planning in various forms, administrative as well as economic. In the field of economic planning strictly so-called, the Commission has drawn up a number of medium-term economic plans intended to provide guidelines to the member-states. The last of these plans, that for the period 1971–1975, endeavoured to give more precise guidance on inflation, unemployment growth rates and balances of payments, but since their implementation is bound up with the controversial issues of monetary and economic unification the medium-term plans have as yet had little real effect. By contrast it might be expected that the Comecon programme would provide a model of clarity and purposeful direction in its discussion of the co-ordination of plans. In fact it does not do so. Basically the question of plan co-ordination is as difficult a political issue (if not more difficult) for Comecon as for the EEC. The new programme totally avoids the question of 'one planner'.

Chapter II of the programme begins with the statement that the member-states will consult each other on basic questions of economic, scientific and technical policy. The consultations will relate 'in particular to those problems which are of importance in these countries' relations with each other': they will be bilateral or multilateral. Bearing in mind the general principle that Comecon integration is 'voluntary', is not accompanied by the creation of supranational organs and does not affect internal planning problems, it is hardly surprising that the recommendations for co-operation in planning are, to say the least, elliptical. The main proposals are for joint forecasting, co-ordination of long-term plans for the most important economic *sectors,* a further *improvement* in the co-ordination of national five-year plans, joint planning by interested countries of *individual branches* of industry, and the co-ordination of capital investment in *production units of common interest.* The central organs of Comecon are to participate 'broadly' in this process and the chairmen of the central planning bodies will co-operate regularly within the framework of Comecon. The question of a single planner does not arise: in its place is an immense network of joint projects, consultation, co-operation, joint services and joint planning systems at all levels from which it will be very difficult for any member-state to extricate itself and within which it will need to defend its own national interest by the exercise of considerable diplomatic skill. The existing differences in national planning methods (a subject never mentioned in the programme) will add to the complexity of the process unless the process itself eliminates them.

On monetary issues both EEC and Comecon appear to be moving —slowly and uncertainly—towards a solution with common elements. The Conference of EEC Heads of State at The Hague in December 1969 agreed that a plan in stages should be worked out during 1970 with a view to creating an economic and monetary union. The implications of this proposal were complete freedom of capital movement, absolutely fixed exchange rates between the currencies of the member-states (or a single currency), and a high degree of harmonisation of economic policies. The Commission submitted proposals, in October 1970, very similar to those of a committee of experts set up under the chairmanship of M. Werner, Prime Minister of Luxembourg, for an economic and monetary union by 1980. It is by no means certain that this objective will be reached by 1980, although a new impetus may have been given by agreement at the EEC 'Summit' meeting in October 1972 to create a full monetary and economic union in the coming decade. The Comecon programme sets out a scheme for achieving a new monetary system in Eastern Europe within the same period. Considering that 'currency, financial and credit relations should play a more active part in . . . the development of socialist integration' the members have agreed to make the transferable rouble the international currency of Comecon with a stable gold content and exchange rate determined by consultation between the member-states. During 1971–1973 the members will extend multilateral accounting with the aid of the transferable rouble, the International Bank for Economic Co-operation and the International Investment Bank (both common institutions within the Comecon framework) will develop new sources of credit, progress will be made towards the establishment of realistic single exchange rates between the national currencies and the transferable rouble (called in the programme 'the collective currency'), and convertibility between the national currencies. 'As its role is strengthened the collective currency (the transferable rouble) may eventually be used in accounts with third countries and occupy, among other currencies employed in the settlement of international accounts, a place corresponding to the role and importance of the Comecon countries in the world economy'. The long-term aim therefore is to make both the collective currency and the national currencies convertible.

The importance of these proposals for the future of East–West relations is very great but at this stage it is enough to point out that monetary unification is the decisive step towards economic integration in a market system and is hardly less so in a planned system. The adoption of common internal and external policies by the group is a *sine qua non* for monetary unification.

The achievement of a common external commercial policy by the EEC at the end of its transitional period in December 1969 was a requirement written into the Treaty of Rome. In addition to the maintenance of a common external tariff and a common agricultural market —neither of which can be modified without collective Community agreement—a common commercial policy also implies Community negotiation of trade agreements, Community management of quantitative import controls, export promotion measures, credit policy and many other aspects of external policy formerly within the competence of the national state. Monetary unification implies a common concern with the Community's balance of payments. In a later chapter it will be shown that some important elements of a common commercial policy especially towards Eastern Europe are still missing but the intention to create one is clear and in due course, probably the later 1970s, it will almost certainly be established in some form. There can be no doubt of the EEC's commitment in principle to this course.

Comecon is not committed by its 1960 statutes to a similar policy; no procedures are laid down for the co-ordination of the external economic policies of its member-states. In practice such informal pressures as the preference for intra-Comecon trade as against trade with third countries have probably exerted a residual influence on the policies of the member-states towards the West, but the whole conception of a common commercial policy as set out in the Treaty of Rome has been strongly criticised in the past by the East European states. The new Comecon programme introduces the idea for the first time: 'the Comecon countries will co-ordinate their foreign economic policy in the interests of normalising international commercial and economic relations, especially with a view to abolishing discrimination in this sphere'. This statement is not further elaborated and no indication is given of the institutional or procedural consequences of a decision to act in common. It is however apparent from the phrasing that the co-ordination of foreign economic policy is not treated, as it is in the Treaty of Rome, as an essential principle of integration but as a means of achieving particular ends, especially 'equal rights for the Socialist states against which discrimination is still being exercised in international economic, scientific and technical organisations'. It might result for example in the establishment of a committee for negotiation with the EEC when the latter's common commercial policy is complete, or in the achievement of a co-ordinated policy among Comecon countries which are, or will be, members of the General Agreement on Tariffs and Trade (GATT). Within the next decade therefore it is probable that joint Comecon negotiating teams will begin to appear on the international scene.

This brief and superficial comparison between EEC and Comecon provides an inadequate basis for a prognostication of the courses they will follow in the next decade. It is clear however a new 'transitional' phase in European economic organisation is opening, with the EEC on the one hand absorbing new members and at the same time trying to bring to fruition the intentions both of the Treaty of Rome and of subsequent decisions of governments to create a closely integrated market which will acquire some, but not all, of the characteristics of a unitary state, and with Comecon, on the other hand, endeavouring through the creation of innumerable new functional arrangements under the governance of a uniform political system to achieve a combination of planning and market elements which will also acquire some, but not all, of the characteristics of a unitary state.

Paradoxically the economic 'philosophy' of the EEC is more easily interpreted than that of Comecon, although the distinction is broadly between a market system modified and supported by elements of indicative planning and a multiple planning system penetrated by elements of market operations. At this point of time, although the general bias of the two organisations—one towards the market and the other towards the plan—is obvious, in neither organisation do market and plan appear as irreconcilable opposites and in the course of a decade or more the balance between plan and market within the two organisations could shift appreciably. The present plans of Comecon are more directly concerned with the mobilisation of resources and the rationalisation of production than are those of the EEC, the assumption in the case of the EEC being that so long as a favourable administrative and economic environment can be provided by Community institutions and procedures, private enterprise should be left to mobilise and utilise resources to the best advantage. In their different ways however both organisations are concerned with the search for optimum scale in industrial and agricultural production.

It may well be that on the EEC side much that is described as 'common policy' will turn out to be 'common procedure' through which the member-states by a system of bargaining and consensus within institutions which are formally 'supranational' will retain the ultimate right of initiative and veto. Within Comecon the member-state is formally guaranteed 'sovereign independence' but if 'integration' is to become a reality elements of sovereignty must be yielded up and supranational institutions (of which a common currency must be reckoned one) at different levels and with perhaps varying durability must come into existence.

3 Communist policy towards West European integration

The Soviet Government refuses to recognise the legal personality of the EEC or to transact business with the Community institutions; unlike most Western states it has no diplomatic representation in Brussels: it has tried by persuasion and a vast output of propaganda to prevent other states from joining the Community; it has criticised almost every aspect of the EEC's activities, from the principles enshrined in the Treaty of Rome to its practical policies. The other Comecon states have followed the Soviet lead in withholding juridical recognition.

The reasons for the Soviet attitude are complex, some deriving from established ideological positions, others from the Soviet view of the political structure of Europe. Although the policy is almost entirely negative and the issue of recognition seemingly one which might be very simply resolved, a change of Soviet policy in this respect would in fact betoken a profound change in the Soviet position on East–West relations, for with recognition would come the practical abandonment of some ideological and political dogmas which still cause suspicion and uneasiness in the West. The consequences of this one act would be very substantial both in the short and the long term.

Whether 'ideology' has served the USSR very well in coming to grips with a new Europe is doubtful. The doctrine, drawn more particularly from Lenin's pamphlet *Imperialism, the Highest Stage of Capitalism,* written in 1916, is that capitalism is now in its last 'imperialist' phase, in which monopoly replaces capitalist free competition. 'Monopoly', says Lenin, 'is the transition from capitalism to a higher system', the last fling of the capitalist system before its eclipse. In strictly ideological terms *all* the organisation of the capitalist world with which the Communist states have to do business are ephemeral *because* they are capitalist. From this it would seem to follow that an integrated Western Europe as a phenomenon of state-monopoly-capitalism is *ipso facto* ephemeral: to establish any relationship with it which might help to prolong its existence and delay the inevitable end would be to interfere with the processes of history.

Since the prophecy of the collapse of capitalism has nothing to say about the probable timing of the event, if offers very little guidance to the practical business of living in peace, or co-existing, with the West. Rather the reverse, since inconclusive theoretical debates about the likelihood or unlikelihood of the collapse of capitalism cause confusion of counsel. This has certainly been proved true in handling the more limited and practical question of the durability of the EEC.

The quotation from Lenin which has been so frequently used by Soviet commentators on the subject of West European integration that it has become threadbare, derives not from 'Imperialism' but from a short paper written in February 1915 entitled *On the Slogan of the United States of Europe*. In it, Lenin, who in 1914 had believed that the creation of a republican United States of Europe would assist the passage of Europe towards socialism, rejected the idea of a federation of Europe *before* it had undergone social transformation. 'Certainly temporary *ententes* between monopolists and between states are possible. In that 'sense the United States of Europe are also possible as an *entente* between European states—but to what end? To the sole end of stifling socialism in Europe and for the common maintenance of oppressed colonies.' On the other hand such *ententes* could not overcome the inner contradictions of monopoly capitalism and were essentially ephemeral.

Lenin's dictum has caused a great deal of trouble in Communist discussion of the process of integration in Western Europe. For while it could be taken for granted that such integration was reactionary it was not so clear that the integrated organisation arising from it was ephemeral. On the whole the USSR itself has tended to adhere to the view, necessary to the theory of imperialism, that Western integration is ephemeral, the validity of the dictum being reasserted by Moscow in the summer of 1971 in commentaries upon the British application to join the EEC. The theme of the inner contradictions of capitalism was given a good airing by Mr. Brezhnev in his speech to the 24th CPSU Congress in May. But the relevance of Lenin's dictum, the central ideological text on Western integration, is limited by the fact that his essay on the United States of Europe was written in the epoch of great European empires—Russian, German, and Austro-Hungarian—when the issue of monarchy versus republic was still a live one, when any association or *entente* between European states could be thought of *only* in political terms. In Lenin's time the concept of economic integration as an end in itself or as a prelude to political integration had not yet appeared. He can hardly be blamed for failing to foresee, at a period of European history which to most of us today seems as remote as the

Middle Ages, what forms the 'internationalisation of production' might take or the types of political association between states to which they might give rise. It is now accepted by the Communist world that the internationalisation of production is an important and permanent characteristic of the modern world, beneficial to the standard of life of the ordinary man and a *sine qua non* for the progress of the states of Eastern Europe themselves. On international association in this form Lenin has nothing relevant to say.

Before the Treaty of Rome came into effect it was confidently predicted, in a document issued by the Institute of World Economy and International Relations, Moscow, in 1957 that the EEC could not overcome its internal contradictions. This document, usually known as the *Seventeen Theses on the Common Market,* survived without criticism for two years only. Between 1959 and 1962 several important conferences of Marxist economists subjected the question of the 'reversibility' or 'irreversibility' of West European integration to searching examination. The result of this debate, in which the Soviet theorreticians modified their views under the pressure of more pragmatic attitudes of mind presented by Marxist economists from Eastern and Western Europe, was another major document, the 'Thirty Two Theses on the Common Market', published in *Pravda* on 26 August 1962. This document and others published at about the same time in Soviet and international Marxist journals recognised that not only had great progress been made in implementing the Treaty of Rome but also that the rate of growth of the EEC was second only to that of Japan in the capitalist world. In a phrase which received wide publicity at the time the Theses declared that the EEC was an 'economic and political reality'. The implication was obvious: the EEC had come to stay. Mr. Khruschchev clearly associated himself with this assessment; he was quoted in the Thirty Two Theses as suggesting that co-operation between the integrated organisations of Western and Eastern Europe should now be considered. Dissimilar as the Seventeen and Thirty Two Theses were in their conclusions, Lenin's dictum found a place in both.

In the year after the publication of the Thirty Two Theses the EEC entered the political crisis precipitated by the French veto on British entry. In 1964 Mr. Khruschchev fell from power and much that he had stood for was discredited. The question whether the EEC was a reality or an 'ephemeral' phenomenon seemed to be open again, the arduous labours of those who had prepared the Theses wasted, the validity of the type of assessment they represented in doubt. No subsequent attempt has been made to produce, by international discussion and consensus, a comparable document essaying a reconciliation between the evidence of contemporary reality and the requirements of doctrine, largely because the views of Communist theoreticians, statesmen and party leaders on the matters dealt with in the Thirty Two Theses have become more rather than less divergent and the relevance of ideology to the whole issue more questionable.

Since 1963 Soviet assessments of the EEC, concerned principally with its potential political significance, have been subject to some changes in emphasis without departing far from the doctrinal theory that as an association between capitalist states the EEC is exceptionally vulnerable to internal contradictions and therefore might, after all, prove to be 'ephemeral' even though the crises through which it has passed have not disrupted its foundation, the customs union. After the first political crisis in the EEC in 1963 and to an even greater extent after the crisis of 1965, Soviet assessments began to discount the possibility of political unification and, placing this internal West European crisis in the context of difficulties in Nato following the French withdrawal, began to regard the EEC as very largely irrelevant to the West European situation. It may very well have been this assessment that accounts for Soviet tolerance of the first Polish moves to make contact with the Brussels Commission in 1964-1965 and to the later contacts established by other East European states. It may also account for the vituperative Soviet reaction to the third British attempt to join the Community in 1971, since the enlargement of the Communities would in any case demonstrate that collapse was not imminent and might even provide a new political initiative.

In more recent years, especially since 1969, the USSR has castigated the EEC as an obstacle to some new form of pan-European order which might be negotiated at a European Security Conference—as an example of the closed and exclusive 'bloc' which must be dissolved if a new European era is to dawn. In other respects Soviet commentaries have been less sure especially in regard to the role of the USA, West Germany and Britain. In the late fifties and early sixties American hegemony linked with West German revanchism was the bogeyman, Britain being represented as a discontented victim of the combination; by contrast the British attempt to join the Community in 1967 was represented as an Anglo-German plot; in 1971 (the Soviet–German pact having been negotiated a year earlier) West Germany was allotted a less villainous role and the British application seen as a 'Trojan horse' operation on behalf of the Americans. Throughout these convolutions however there were two constants, closely related to one another, (a) refusal to 'recognise' the Community and (b) insistence on the Community's internal contradictions. Together they appear to represent a belief that the withholding of recognition might even yet contribute to stagnation in the Community's political evolution. Perhaps equally important, they might serve to discourage others in Eastern Europe from seeking new working relationships witth Brussels.

Like the USSR itself the non-Russian states of Comecon have withheld juridical recognition from the EEC. To this day they criticise the EEC as a closed and exclusive group dominated by monopolies. But unlike the USSR several of these states, with high foreign trade dependence and important commercial exchanges with the West European states, view the existence of the EEC's Common Agricultural Policy (CAP) and Common External Tariff (CET) with concern. If they are to sell agricultural products to the EEC they must in fact take cognisance of the CAP and seek to minimise its effects. There is of course nothing in Leninism or in modern Soviet doctrine which prohibits trade between socialist and capitalist countries, nor are these states bound by the statutes of Comecon to co-ordinate their trade policies towards the West or with the USSR. In the 1960s they were still enjoying the liberty of action conferred by the post-Stalin doctrine of separate roads to socialism proclaimed by Khruschchev at the 20th Congress of the Soviet Communist Party in 1956 and afterwards. Unless the USSR was to impair their economic progress it had to exercise tolerance for policies which might diverge somewhat from its own. In consequence differences of national attitudes and policies between the non-Russian states of Comecon towards the EEC have long been apparent.

East Germany, not recognised as a state by the members of the EEC but comfortably tucked in between the internal German market on one side and a rapidly growing Soviet market for its industrial products on the other, could afford to follow the Soviet political line on thee EEC very closely and under Ulbricht was consistently hostile. More recently however attacks upon the Community have diminished.

Poland from the outset was more moderate in its criticism of the EEC than the USSR and the main weight of Polish objections was to the economic rather than the political aspects of Western integration. As early as 1959 Poland applied for membership of the General Agreement on Tariffs and Trade, a sign of its desire for closer relations with the world trading system, and it was the first of the Comecon states to approach the EEC Commission and thereby recognise, *de facto,* its existence. In November 1964 the Poles, insisting that their action did not amount to recognition, entered into negotiations with the Commission and in 1965 concluded an agreement exempting EEC imports of Polish eggs from supplementary levies under the common agricultural policy. A further agreement concluded in Marrch 1968 covered her export of poultry and pig-meat to the Community. The British application to join the EEC is of considerable importance to Poland, since the UK is one of Poland's chief trading partner in Western Europe. But Polish comments on British accession have been mild and whhile apprehensive about the possible economic consequences by no means hostile politically. The Polish attitude to the EEC remains as it has been for the most part from the beginning, a pragmatic one designed to make the best of a 'reality' which the Poles have never seriously questioned.

Hungary reacted to the creation of the EEC cautiously. In February 1968 the Prime Minister, Mr. Jëno Fock, reminding his hearers that the EEC was a reality, said that 'if our economic relations demand that we should approach one of the Common Market organisations in Brussels, we shall not regard this as a renunciation of our principles'. In April and June 1968 'technical discussions' between Hungary and the EEC Commission leading to a similar agreement to that concluded by Poland was concluded by an exchange of letters between Hungary and the Commission. In a report to thee Hungarian Parliament in July 1968, Mr. Janos Peter, the Minister for Foreign Affairs, said that Hungary was prepared to 'study the possibilities of a broad European co-operation with the office of the Common Market'. In July 1969 Mr. Josef Biro, Minister of Foreign Trade, said that if the members of the EEC were to surrender decision-making on matters of trade to the central institutions of the Communities, Hungary was ready to conclude agreements with those institutions regarding the export of certain Hungarian products. The enlargement of the EEC was discussed objectively by the Hungarian press and radio as British accession became more certain. Like the Poles the Hungarians take a practical rather than an ideological view of West European integration.

Until the overthrow of Mr. Dubček in May 1969, the Czechoslovak attitude to the EEC was comparatively objective. As one of the two most highly industrialised non-Russian members of Comecon (East Germany being the other) Czechoslovakia was esspecially concerned with the common external tariff of the EEC and with quota restrictions. During the reform period (the 'Prague Spring') the Dubček –Cernik government did not depart from the impeccably orthodox line that while remaining a member of the socialist commonwealth it was seeking improved economic relations with the West (in this hardly differing at all from Poland and Hungary) and reserved the right to decide in the national interest how to deal with the community institutions of the EEC. As the conservatives regained authority in the Czechoslovak party during 1969 the orthodox Soviet line on the EEC began to reappear in Czechoslovak commentaries and for the time being the distinctive Czechoslovak voice in the discussion fell silent.

Rumanian criticism of the EEC has fastened upon the supranational element in the Treaty of Rome. Clearly influenced by its own national resistance to supranationalism within Comecon, the Rumanian government has repeatedly rejected the EEC as a model for Eastern Europe. However, in 1969 the Rumanians followed the Polish example and concluded an agreement with the EEC by an exchange of letters whereby, in return for accepting the Community's sluice-gate prices, they were granted exemption from supplementary levies on a range of their agricultural products. In March 1972 the Rumanians asked for negotiations for a trade agreement with the EEC to be put in train.

The success of Yugoslavia's arrangements with the EEC must serve to reinforce the pragmatic attitudes of non-Russian members of Comecon. A formal trade agreement came into effect in 1970 and Yugoslav trade with the Community expanded considerably in that year and in 1971. At the same time Yugoslavia began to benefit from co-operation with the EEC in science and technology.

The Chinese, who in 1962 disliked the EEC and opposed the conclusions of the Thirty Two Theses on the grounds that they were 'revisionist', now accept the fact of the EEC's existence and regard West European unity as a valuable counter to the influence of the USA and the USSR. The Chinese government is anxious to develop trade with the Community.

To the diversity of views on the EEC now held by Communist governments must be added differences between West European Communist Parties. The drafting of the Thirty Two Theses in 1962 owed a great deal to the influence of the Italian Communist Party, which had reached the conclusion that to remain in opposition to the EEC was not only to fly in the face of the evident fact that it had already conferred benefits upon the Italian worker but also to throw away any chance of exerting a political influence in the EEC's community institutions. The French Communist Party at first held the contrary view but moved progressively closer to the Italians. The Thirty Two Theses, by accepting the 'reality' of the EEC, could logically go on to indicate to the Communist Parties of the EEC member-states a programme for the 'reform' of the EEC from within. This the document did by calling for opposition to the monopolies, nationalisation of EEC industries and the opening up of Community institutions to progreessive political forces. This programme was endorsed by a meeting of the Communist Parties of the EEC at a meeting in Brussels in March 1963.

It had been proved that no massive political opposition to the establishment of the EEC such as that called for by the Seventeen Theses of 1957 could be organised by the Communists. In the new situation, when the reality of the EEC's existence had been acknowledged, the main burden of the task of reforming or transforming the Community from within must fall upon the shoulders of the two large Communist-dominated trade union confederations, the CGT in France and the CGIL in Italy, who between them organised more than a quarter of the labour force of the EEC. The two confederations established a joint liaison bureau in Brussels in 1967 and in April 1969 the EEC Commission agreed to establish contact with it. The CGT and CGIL obtained a small representation on the Economic and Social Committee. But to the CGIL in particular effective action at the Community level could only be achieved if the non-Communist unions of the EEC, the majority of which belong to the International Confederation of Free Trade Unions or to the World Confederation of Labour, could be induced to form a common front with the two Communist-dominated confederations, especially if collective bargaining could be moved from the national to the Community level. A major obstacle to such a common front is the adherence of both the CGT and CGIL to the Communist World Federation of Trade Unions (WFTU). CGIL came to the conclusion in 1968 that to provide a basis for joint action it was necessary to create a new 'non-political' regional grouping of West European trade unions. It presented its case at the 7th Congress of WFTU in 1969 and found itself in a minority of one, the 'official' view, strongly backed by the Soviet and East European delegates, being that regionalism of the type proposed by the Italians would undermine the world role of WFTU. The CGT voted with the majority. The problem remains unresolved. WFTU membership must continue to hamper both CGIL and CGT in their search for a common front with the other EEC unions but there is no sign of a recognition of this fact on the part of WFTU.

While the Communist Parties of the EEC have come to terms with the EEC in the sense that they accept the existence of the EEC community institutions and are unable to show that membership of the EEC has operated to the disadvantage of the workers of the member-states, the Communist Parties of the candidate countries continue (in 1972) to oppose the accession of Britain, Ireland, Denmark and Norway.

All in all, dialectical materialism as an intellectual system has not been equal to the task of establishing a common position towards West European integration among the Communist Parties of the world and it is difficult to see what, if anything, the Parties have gained from discussing the issue in ideological terms.

The political case against West European integration is no less shaky than the ideological case. If the argument with which Chapter 1 of this book opens is accepted it is totally meaningless to describe West European integration as a 'Cold War manoeuvre'. Having subscribed to the conclusions of the Thirty Two Theses that the EEC was a political and economic reality the Soviet government then proceeded to act as if in fact it did not exist while maintaining a stream of propaganda based on the assumption that it not only did exist, but was highly dangerous. The maintenance of this hostile but equivocal attitude for so long has done very little to hamper the development of the EEC and nothing whatever to deter the candidate states from making their application to join. Fulminations about 'neocolonialism' have not prevented developing countries from assoociating themselves with the EEC nor have denunciations of the evils of 'blocs' prevented the conclusion of an agreement between Yugoslavia and the Community. Whereas until 1970 some political capital might be made of the dominant position of Western Germany in the EEC—for long one of the bogeymen of Soviet propaganda—the signature of the German–Soviet Pact in May 1972, the easing of German–Soviet tensions and the moderation of East European attitudes towards Federal Germany resulting from it has created a situation in which it is no longer sensible to play upon fears of German 'revanchism'. It is clear that although France is prepared to further Franco–Soviet commercial and technological exchanges and to maintain friendly relations with Moscow, it is not to be detached from the West. Every effort on the part of the Russians to persuade British governments that it would be disastrous for them to join the EEC has failed. The economic and social case against membership on the grounds that the working classes of the member-states will suffer is contrary to the facts and does not even appeal to Italian or French Communists. On all these counts the Soviet case against the EEC is crumbling rapidly and persistence in opposition serves no purpose except to arouse Western suspicions of Soviet motives.

Only one rational ground for Soviet immobilism now remains. It is that before the new structure of Western Europe is finally accepted in Moscow it may just be possible to offer Europe as a whole a Continent-wide system of security and economic interdependence attractive enough to give rise to second thoughts in Western capitals about the consolidation of their own political and economic structure. The possibility is in fact a remote one but Soviet diplomatic activity in Europe in 1971–1972 suggests that the USSR considers the attempt worthwhile, especially as it would receive the unanimous support of East European governments and West European Communist Parties.

The economic content of this policy made its first appearance at the Spring session of the Economic Commission for Europe (ECE) of the United Nations at Geneva in 1956. The USSR submitted to the session a set of broad proposals for co-operation between all European states, a government note to the ECE Secretariat and a draft agreement on co-operation. Beginning with a general declaration in favour of respect for sovereign rights and non-interference in internal affairs, the draft went on to propose in general terms the proliferation of bilateral or multilateral trade agreements between the states of Eastern and Western Europe, multilateral payments arrangements, bilateral agreements on transport and joint utilisation of natural resources. These proposals were referred to in the Seventeen Theses on the Common Market published in 1957 and were from the first associated in the minds of Western governments with Soviet opposition to the establishment of the

EEC as a new West European preferential system. The pronouncements of the Soviet government and treatment of the question in the Soviet press made it quite clear that the proposals for co-operation were offered as an alternative to Western integration.

The proposals were repeated and somewhat elaborated by the USSR at the 1957, 1958 and 1959 ECE sessions. In 1960 proposals for joint planning and building of industrial projects, a conference of foreign trade Ministers, the expansion of scientific and technical collaboration were added. Throughout the period the USSR appeared to have in mind the creation of some kind of regional trade organisation for Europe.

On this general approach, with its avoidance of doctrinal issues, there has been general agreement on the Communist side. The theme has been constantly repeated for over a decade and is associated with proposals for a European security conference.

In so far as the approach is a sign of a desire for *détente* in Europe it is to be welcomed and no doubt Soviet proposals will be listened to at a security conference with at least the same degree of attention that they received ten years ago in Geneva. On the other hand it has never been clear that these proposals either introduce new methods or techniques into East–West relations or indeed whether they have evolved significantly since they were first made. There has in fact been a considerable expansion of trade and technical co-operation between the countries of Western and Eastern Europe since 1960, limited partly by differences between the two economic systems, partly by differences in the level of economic development between Western and Eastern Europe, and partly by hesitation arising from political malaise.

In the West it is not easy to forget that the initiation of the Soviet proposals coincided with the last stages of the work of M. Spaak's Committee which laid the foundations of the EEC and that they were expressly linked, as they still are, with Soviet opposition to the EEC. Whatever their positive merit it has been clouded by this fact. Doubts on the subject of the intention which may lie behind the proposals have never been lightened by any suggestion that major concessions would be made on the East European side. Although much has been said about the sins of closed blocs in Europe (and Mr. Brezhnev said a great deal on this subject during his visit to Paris in October 1971) no suggestion has ever been made by the USSR that the programme for the integration of Comecon should be modified in favour of a pan-European structure. Rather the contrary, for Soviet policy in that area clearly favours a much more closely integrated East European system. The Soviet view seems to be that Comecon is not negotiable whereas the EEC is negotiable, which suggests serious limitations to the Soviet negotiating position and is hardly encouraging from a Western point of view.

The Soviet proposals have always been imprecise. They have been cast in such a form that while no Western state anxious for *détente* could object to them in principle, it has not been possible to discern what, in purely economic terms, is new in them. On the whole, since they have for the most part been concerned with long-term bilateral economic agreements and planned projects, they have, for all their references to multilateralism, looked much more like the extension of the Comecon system to the rest of Europe than a new start. Moreover the USSR itself has made no suggestion that its own state-trading system should be modified in any way so as to bring it closer to the trading methods of Western Europe.

While there is room for reasonable doubt about the precise economic purposes of the Soviet proposals there can be little doubt about their political purpose. While the USSR has studiously ignored the existence of the Community institutions in Brussels it has initiated from its own side and quickly responded to any initiative from the Western side for closer bilateral relations with the member-states of the EEC. Useful though the improvement of bilateral arrangements are they inevitably conflict to a greater or less extent with the concept of a common West European approach to East–West relations and, as will be seen later, have contributed somewhat to the EEC's difficulties in searching for a common policy. Both the West German government during its negotiations for a pact with the USSR in 1970 and the French government in its negotiations with Mr. Brezhnev in 1971 seem to have made it clear to the Russians that improved relations with the USSR are not to be taken as implying a disregard of the obligations of these states to their Western partnerships.

As the time for the holding of a European Security Conference, at which the attitude of the USSR towards the integration of Western Europe will undoubtedly come under public scrutiny, draws nearer the difficulties of the Soviet position become more apparent. In the early months of 1972 different Soviet voices could be heard, some rigidly orthodox, others quavering on the verge of change. In January 1972 Moscow Radio was still clinging to the conception of pan-Europeanism as an *alternative* to Western integration, asserting that the enlargement of the Common Market would create additional obstacles to pan-European co-operation. The old complaint that Nato was trying to use the Common Market as the economic base for a military bloc was given yet another airing. In March however Mr. Brezhnev, speaking at the 15th Soviet Trade Union Congress, seemed to strike a slightly different note. He said that the USSR is observing the activities and development of the Common Market 'with interest' and that Soviet relations *with the EEC countries* (my italics: not, it is to be noted, with the Community institutions) will depend on the extent to which they recognise 'the reality of what exists in the Socialist part of Europe, and in particular the interests of the Comecon member countries'. He went on to say that the idea that the USSR wishes to undermine the EEC is 'absurd': the Common Market is part of the existing situation in Western Europe. Mr. Brezhnev's statement is of course of interest but his treatment of the theme of Soviet relations with the EEC is akin to that of Mr. Khruschchev in 1962. In 1962 the 'reality' of the EEC had already been recognised in the Thirty Two Theses and elsewhere, but basing his proposals for economic co-operation between EEC and Comecon upon that 'reality' Mr. Khruschchev spoke only of relations between the member-states of the two organisations, not specifically of the Community institutions. In this respect Mr. Brezhnev's statement does not advance beyond Mr. Khruschchev's. It has also to be looked at in the context of the German–Soviet Treaty. In March 1972 the balance for and against ratification of the Treaty in the German Parliament was so close that there seemed to be an equal chance that it would succeed or fail. In December 1971 Dr. Barzel, the leader of the Christian Democrat Party, which was opposing ratification, visited Moscow and in the course of his discussions urged recognition of the EEC. He obtained no response. By March however Moscow realised that anything which could shift Christian Democrat opinion might tip the scales in favour of ratification of the Treaty. In this context it seems that the main audience intended for Mr. Brezhnev's remarks about the EEC was in Bonn. It will not be possible to assess their real significance until, or unless, they are repeated for a wider audience and in other circumstances.

When the USSR has to reconsider its refusal to recognise the existence of the Community institutions of the EEC the doctrinal issue will emerge again. It is unlikely that this decision will be forced upon the USSR in the immediate future unless it is an undisclosed concession that the USSR might be prepared to make for bargaining purposes at a European Security Conference, but if the enlargement of the Communities does in fact give new life to the search for common policies the EEC could reach a point at which it would be strong and coherent enough to withhold economic negotiations with Eastern Europe unless they are conducted through Community channels. The EEC needs to overcome many internal difficulties of its own before it can be strong enough to take a stand and bargain economic advantage against political recognition in this way. And in the present climate the EEC would obviously be reluctant to force such a confrontation. Assuming that such a point can be reached however it will present the USSR with certain dilemmas. To recognise the EEC would in the first place be to grant that it is a permanent and stable organisation. This would deal a blow at the theory that as a phenomenon of state-monopoly capitalism it must collapse under the pressure of its own internal contradictions; it would make nonsense of this doctrinal element in the long anti-EEC campaign. Secondly, it would make nonsense of the long-sustained Soviet attack on the 'supranationalism' of the Treaty of Rome and the organisation of the EEC. On this issue it is interesting to speculate whether the USSR would for long have sustained itss hostility to the EEC if it had immediately adopted a federal political structure and become in effect a single large state overnight. Here Lenin could not have helped, since he believed in the virtues of very large states. Be that as it may, to recognise the EEC of the Treaty of Rome would be to accept its special form of supranationalism.

These are possible doctrinal dilemmas arising from recognition. The others are practical. Recognition would inevitably mean that the Soviet plan for a pan-European system of economic relations as an *alternative* to Western integration had failed. It would also mean that Brussels as the 'capital' of the largest and most powerful economic grouping in Western Europe with a network of overseas associations would become the centre of East–Westt negotiations in Europe, thereby not only enhancing the status of the Community institutions but acting as a magnet to other countries.

It is idle to pretend that it will be easy for the USSR, which regards itself as the guardian of Marx–Leninism and in some sense the champion of the theory of enduring class-war in international relattions, to abandon much of its position at one stroke with a few graceful and deprecatory gestures. But unless (a) the EEC fails for internal reasons to establish satisfactory procedures for conducting its relations with Eastern Europe on a common basis or (b) the USSR within the next two or three years can present practical, alternative proposals for pan-European co-operation which are, and can manifestly be seen to be, more advantageous to the EEC member-states than the development of their own 'community' relationships, the USSR will need to accept West European integration as an 'irreversible' fact, recognise the institutions of the EEC and start afresh with the elaboration of methods of doing business with it. Another four or five years may pass before this situation is reached, a period long enough to allow the USSR to discard gradually, and without embarrassment, at least some of the grounds for its previous hostility. By the mid or later 1970s the USSR will need to reach an accommodation of some kind with the enlarged EEC as an entity. Such an accommodation will not necessarily spell the end to ideological differences or reconcile opposing visions of the 'ultimate' structure of the European continent but it will go a long way towards removing the obstacles created by such visions from the practical conduct of affairs. There is no reason to suppose that an enlarged

EEC would fail to respond in a flexible and pragmatic way to the change in the Soviet posture.

4 EEC attitudes and policies towards Eastern Europe

The common policy of the EEC *regarded as a unit* towards Eastern Europe must be deduced from the decisions of the Council of Ministers, arrived at by the 'Community method' of drafting policy documents in the Commission for discussion and decision by the Council. In this process the Commission is guided by the requirements of the Treaty of Rome on the one hand and on the other by its assessment of the attitude and policies of the member-states. The Commission as a Community institution is charged under Article 155 of the Treaty with ensuring that the provisions of the Treaty are carried out. The Council, composed of representatives of the member-states, is given the broader and less clearly defined role of ensuring that the economic policies of the member-states are co-ordinated. It is at the Council level that the national policies of the member-states are fully brought to bear upon the proposals and decisions of the Commission and from the interplay between the Commission representing the Treaty and the Council representing the policies of national states emerges the consensus of views which is the common policy.

The Treaty of Rome is of course concerned with commercial policy and not with foreign policy in general, but commercial decisions in all countries of the world are influenced by political considerations: political influences upon trade policy are none the less strong for being undeclared: foreign trade policies have enduring political consequences. The Commission in attempting to implement those provisions of the Treaty of Rome which relate to external commercial policy is involved in an important aspect of foreign policy which, in its widest sense, remains the prerogative of the governments of the member-states. A beginning is now being made, in the context of the enlargement of the Community with the establishment of new political institutions independent of the Commission and the Treaty, within which it may be possible in the course of time to arrive at collective community views on general foreign policy issues. Instructed by the meeting of the Heads of Government of the Six in December 1969, a Committee of the political directors of the foreign ministries drew up the 'Davignon Plan' for regular consultation between the member-states on foreign policy within which harmonisation of points of view and, where possible, common policies might be achieved. A political secretariat, principally to service the periodic meetings of the Foreign Ministers of member-countries is being established. The EEC summit meeting in October 1972 did not attempt to tackle major issues of political structure in the enlarged Community, but agreed that the Foreign Ministers of the Nine States should in future meet four times a year. These somewhat hesitant exploratory moves towards political unification are a recognition of the fact that the EEC has lacked a common political attitude towards many major issues of external policy, not least towards Eastern Europe.

The Treaty of Rome makes no specific reference to the Communist world or even to state-trading countries, and although it refers to commercial *'policy'* what it in fact requires is the establishment of *procedures* for reaching policies, giving no hint of what the policy should be except in the general sense that its first concern is with the impact of external relations upon the *internal* affairs of the Community. External factors are inevitably considered in the light of their possible relevance to the process of completing the internal process of integration.

The governments of the member-states of the EEC and its central institutions of course share important elements of a common 'ideology', taking the word to mean a complete system of ideas. Whether they incline towards socialist or conservative views about the role of the state in the management of the economy and the distribution of its product among the citizens of the state, they hold very similar views about the liberty of the individual, political institutions and democratic processes, pluralism of political parties, freedom of choice for the consumer and in varying degrees a respect for the virtues of competition within a modified market economy. The Six founding states, and the new entrants also, derive attitudes and policies from the wider Western political system and the predominantly Western international organisations to which they belong. The 'ideology' of the Nine allows for considerable latitude in establishing political positions and is markedly different from that of the 'Socialist Commonwealth' of Eastern Europe in three important respects. In the first place, there is no 'official' political doctrine to which members are required to subscribe (although this is a generalisation which has not yet been put to a severe test, for no member-state has yet deviated into authoritarianism of the extreme right or left). Secondly, the member governments do not have any very precise vision of the 'ultimate' social and political structure which is to emerge from their policies (as against this however it cannot be said that the 'ultimate' goal of full Communism is a very precise concept either). According to the policy of the governing party, and responding to changing public opinion, governments have a general sense of what is better or worse in the short term, but are unwilling to impose policies which may be held to be for the long-term public good against the run of public opinion. Thirdly, they have no 'historicist' view of social and political evolution on a world-wide scale comparable to that of Marx–Leninism. There is among the Nine no official or even generally accepted view, for example, about the future of socialism in Eastern Europe comparable with the Marx–Leninist view that capitalism *must* collapse and be replaced by socialism or that international class-war is a permanent feature of the international scene. Governments are therefore not required either to justify their actions in ideological terms or to handle their relations with Eastern Europe on the assumption that the East European form of socialism is an ephemeral phenomenon doomed by the process of history to collapse and be replaced by capitalism. The Six have already enjoyed the advantage of freedom from this kind of ideological clutter in shaping their policies and the Nine will be equally fortunate.

In its earliest years the EEC paid little attention to Eastern Europe, but dangers were seen by the Commission in the relations between member-states and Eastern Europe. In the first place if member-states conducted their relations on a purely bilateral basis with East European states the Community could suffer the adverse effects to be feared from East European trading practices. In the second place bilateralism and the pursuit of divergent national policies on the part of the member-states could prevent the integration of the Community into an economic union.

The Commission began its search for the general basis of a common policy towards Eastern Europe in 1959–1960, by discussing with the member-states the question of relations with countries having abnormally low producer prices or conducting their trade by state trading methods. On 25 July 1959 the Economic and Social Committee expressed the opinion that failure to co-ordinate commercial policy *vis-à-vis* these countries and also countries operating multiple rates of exchange 'or other practices calculated to distort prices artificially' could wreck free trade in certain industrial and agricultural products within the Community because the provisions of Article 115 of the Treaty would enable member-states during the transition period to take unco-ordinated protective measures of their own. Clearly the states of Eastern Europe came within the category of states against which a Community 'defence' had to be found, although they were not named.

In 1960 the first steps towards an EEC policy came into conflict with that of the USSR and other Eastern European countries, on the subject of the duration of trade agreements. Whereas the USSR favoured the conclusion of *long-term* bilateral agreements between European states, the Commission of the EEC, mindful of its commitment to establish a common policy for the community, argued that bilateral agreements should be *short-term* so that the system of negotiating them could be made flexible. On 20 July 1960 the Coucil of Ministers agreed that in negotiating trade agreements with third countries member-states should seek to include a clause providing for amendment of the agreements should the gradual establishment of a common commercial policy make it necessary.

This clause, known as the 'EEC Clause', was intended, firstly, to introduce the concept of the Community as a juridical entity into agreements with third countries, and secondly to ensure that the internal difficulties already encountered in establishing a common commercial policy should not be increased by the existence of bilateral agreements with inflexible time-limits. The Comecon countries took exception to this clause as a device to secure from them a 'recognition' of the Community and also on the grounds that it put their bilateral agreements with EEC countries at the mercy of internal developments in the Community. While acquiescing in the annexation of the clause to commercial treaties they did not formally recognise its juridical status.

On 9 October 1961 the Council decided to establish a systematic procedure for prior consultation on all provisions of commercial agreements, limited the duration of trade agreements to the transition period of the Treaty (i.e. the end of 1969) and decided that any agreements which included neither the EEC clause nor a clause providing for denunciation from year to year were to be limited to a duration of one year only. It is improbable that these EEC decisions were deliberately discriminatory against Eastern Europe as such: their primary purpose was to restrain the member-states of the EEC from entering into agreements which would hinder the establishment of an EEC common commercial policy.

From the earliest years of the EEC it was evident that the credit policies of the separate states towards Eastern Europe might conflict with the concept of a common commercial policy. The Community therefore set up a Group to co-ordinate financial measures in support of exports in September 1960. Its function was to secure collaboration between national authorities responsible for guarantees and financial credits exceeding the five years permitted by the Berne Union of Credit Insurers. By July 1961 it had been accepted by member-states that they would consult together before giving guarantees connected with the supply of goods if the period of credit proposed was more than five years. The consultation arrangements, after approval by the Council, came into effect at the end of May 1962. In the course of 1963 these arrangements helped to establish the habit of consultation between member-states and to create permanent contacts between credit insurers in the member countries and between member governments; but they did not produce a Community policy.

Between 1961 and 1966 EEC countries granted the Comecon countries fourteen major credits amounting to $225 million, the credit periods varying from 6 to 10 years. Other countries outside the Community granted 59 loans totalling $346 million, for periods between $5\frac{1}{2}$ and 11 years. It was evident from these figures that (a) the members of the Community were themselves exceeding the terms of the Berne Union and (b) that non-members were exceeding them still more.

British action in providing cover by the British Exports Credits Guarantee Department for a loan of 15 years' duration for the Soviet purchase of a polyester fibre plant in September 1964 led to a further examination of Community credit policy. The EEC Council of Ministers discussed the situation in September 1964, largely on the insistence of the German government. The German view was that an extension of the five-year limit for credit would not only lead to undesirable competition among member-states but would also encourage the East Europe countries to compete more effectively in the less-developed countries of the world. They were supported in their stand by the Commission and the Dutch. France objected to the apparent preference enjoyed by the UK in obtaining contracts in the USSR by reason of its ability to offer long-term credit terms. In 1964 and 1965 the member-states of the EEC unilaterally liberalised their own credit policies towards Eastern Europe and when the subject was discussed in March 1966 it was in the aftermath of the 1965 crisis in the EEC. On this occasion M. Couve de Murville argued that, as the granting of credits was an act of foreign policy, unless or until a Community foreign policy could be established the credit question was not within the competence of the Community at all. No agreement was reached apart from a decision to call for further study, and to limit credits to East Germany to five years.

Little progress was made in the harmonisation of export credits until October 1970 when two directives were adopted providing for common standards on insurance for medium and long-term credits, but the question of a common policy in regard to the volume and duration of credits to Eastern Europe has not been finally resolved and is unlikely to be resolved until well on into the 1970s. The issue still remains essentially political; there is no evidence that East European borrowers are uncreditworthy and no economic criterion has yet been established by which to judge whether the grant of credits is 'too large' except the capacity of East European borrowers to service and repay their debts. An effective 'community' credit policy implies the virtual pooling of EEC resources and the offer of uniform terms, so that monetary unification may be the essential preliminary to a common policy in this field.

The interests of the member-states in regard to the supply of energy within the Community have also been divergent. In 1959 there was a crisis in the energy market in the Community, an abundance of oil supplies increasing the difficulty of selling coal and causing a fall in the prices of petroleum products. Imports of petroleum from Comecon countries, particularly the USSR, were rising. Since each government took its own measures to meet the national situation wide gaps appeared between fuel oil prices in the member-states. The need to establish a common market in oil had become pressing. An Inter-Executive Working Party on Energy was set up to examine the situation and make proposals, for it was recognised that the differences in fuel oil prices between member-states could cause major divergences in costs and so compromise the achievement of the common market in general. It was also recognised that the creation of a common market in oil would involve the establishment of a common trade policy towards non-member countries. Among the non-member countries the USSR was considered to require particular attention 'because imports are concentrated at a small number of points and because of the freedom of manoeuvre enjoyed by the USSR in respect of prices'.

The Ministers of the Six meeting in Rome on 6 March 1962 instructed the Executives of the three European Communities to submit a study and proposals for an energy policy to the Special Council of Ministers of ECSC. A Memorandum containing the Executives' proposals was sent to the Council on 27 June 1962. It proposed that there should be free movement of crude oil and petroleum products throughout the Community, free import of crude oil and petroleum products from non-member countries and community quotas for imports from East European countries.

The intention of these proposals in so far as they concerned the Comecon countries was clearly to establish Community control of the import of oil and petroleum products.

Although a consultative procedure among member-states has apparently been adhered to, it is clear from the subsequent history of the debate on energy policy that it has not resolved fundamental differences of interest. In October 1963 the European Parliament debated the subject, approved the main lines of the Memorandum and regretted that the Councils of the three Communities had not shown sufficient political strength of purpose to take decisions on it. Another Special Committee was set up and reported its findings in November 1963 to the ECSC Council, which failed to agree. In January 1964 Parliament again criticised a lack of resolution and purpose in the Council, with very little result. A 'protocol of agreement' relating to energy problems was adopted in April 1964 by the representatives of the member-states within the ECSC Special Council of Ministers but this did little more than express the conviction that a common energy market must ultimately be established.

In 1968 the energy working group of the Commission proposed the first guidelines for a common energy policy based upon the principles of fair competition, low-cost supply, security and freedom of choice for the consumer and stability of supply in respect of cost and quantity, but although the Council of Ministers approved the principles in 1969 little progress has been made, apart from the adoption by the Council of Ministers in February 1972 of the principle that member-states should pool information on oil imports and investment projects. As a result the special form of common policy towards Eastern Europe proposed in 1962 has not come into effect. The issue was avoided at the Summit meeting of the Nine in October 1972.

In the agricultural sector prices are protected at the Community frontier to prevent non-member states with low export prices from gaining any advantage in the Community market but imports are free from quantitative limitations such as quotas, subject to the condition that the Council has the right to decide otherwise if necessary. State trading countries were however subject to special conditions from 1963 onwards, which rendered their agricultural exports liable to quantitative control.

On 24 January 1963 the Council decided to authorise member-states to avail themselves provisionally of the right to waive the principle of liberalisation in respect of the countries of Eastern Europe. Regulation 3/63/CEE, which incorporated this decision, permitted the removal of quantitative restrictions on the import of grain, pigmeat, poultrymeat, eggs, fruit, vegetables and wine from the state trading countries but provided that this should be accompanied by a system of control and suspension in the event of 'a disturbance of the market'. A Community procedure was to be instituted if annual imports exceeded average imports for 1960-1961 by more than 20% and the market in one or more member-countries was, or threatened to be, seriously disturbed. The system was extended to milk, beef, veal and rice on 31 July 1964, thus covering virtually the whole of East European agricultural exports to the Community, and was renewed annually. The reason given for this form of discrimination was first, that the state trading countries practise price manipulation, and second, that trade relations with these countries are conducted under strictly bilateral conditions and are based upon reciprocal granting of quotas, in this respect being in conflict with the multilateral nature of the Community's agricultural policy towards other non-member states.

As the transition period drew to its end the Commission of the Community became sensitive to criticisms of the discriminatory character of Regulation 3/63/CEE and in July 1967 drew up proposals to eliminate it. In fact the Regulation had never been used. In its recommendations to the Council the Commission held that in view of the progress made in the field of agricultural policy and 'the evolving attitudes of the member-states and the Community regarding commerce with the state-trading countries' it was now desirable to extend the rules to other products and to cease to apply them exclusively to the state trading countries. These proposals represented a cautious adjustment of policy to accommodate changing political attitudes.

Because agricultural exports from Eastern Europe are a major balancing item in trade exchanges between the EEC and Eastern Europe, the Commission conducted unofficial negotiations with Poland in 1964–1965, and with Hungary, Rumania and Bulgaria in 1969 whereby those countries were enabled to export a range of agricultural products to the EEC free of supplementary levies at the frontier.

One specifically 'Community' policy towards Eastern Europe operating in the transition period remains to be mentioned. Since 1963 the European Coal and Steel Community has retained control over the volume of imports of iron and steel from state trading countries and has forbidden ECSC producers to align prices on low quotations from East European countries.

The severity of this control is however being slowly relaxed. In 1971 the European Coal and Steel Community (since 1967 'fused' with the EEC at the Commission level) modified the 1963 regulations in order to liberalised four 'not particularly sensitive' groups of steel products. More groups were to be liberalised in 1972. In this sector, where discrimination specifically against Eastern Europe has been in force, a more liberal era seems to be drawing.

It will be seen that the position from which attempts to secure a common policy towards Eastern Europe began was that (a) common external policies were necessary in order to protect the EEC from *internal* distortions—a principle applying to relations with all third countries but with perhaps special force to state-trading countries; (b) the Common Market needed to be protected against special dangers arising from the trading practices of the East European states and possibly—although this was never made explicit—against 'undue' dependence on East European supplies. Partly because these attempts were frustrated by conflicts of interest between the member-states but partly because the community method, ponderous though it is, is sufficiently flexible to allow changes in foreign policy attitudes to work their way through the decision-making process, the EEC came out of the transition period in 1969 without creating a discriminatory *community* policy towards Eastern Europe. The highly 'defensive' attitude which persisted up to about 1964 gradually gave way in response to initiatives by the member-states to a more 'open' attitude towards Eastern Europe. Now the Community institutions, notably the Commission, may appear by reason of insistence on common policies to be conservative as against the more liberal attitudes of the member-states but it is important to understand, in relation to future developments, that the attitude of the Commission was determined by its concern for the internal implementation of the Treaty and not by some independent 'policy' of its own towards Eastern Europe.

From 1966 onwards, partly in response to an improvement in the political atmosphere and partly to meet difficulties in the trading position, the member-states, led by France, began to liberalise their imports from Eastern Europe. Britain, from outside the Community, provided an impulse to the process of liberalisation when in 1964 quotas were replaced in British trade with Poland, Czechoslovakia, Rumania, Hungary and Bulgaria by open general licences matching undertakings on the East European side to align their prices on those offered in the world market. The EEC members did not generally adopt this principle for their own trade with Eastern Europe but immediately followed the French in 1966 in abolishing a considerable part of their existing import quotas. By February 1967, of the 1097 positions of the EEC common external tariff, France had abolished quotas on 817 for East European countries, West Germany 650, Benelux 1024 and Italy 200. By the first half of 1968 the French list had increased to 880 (75% of its trade with the USSR and East Europe), the Italian had increased to 840 (80%), the West German to 50–60% (the principal items still remaining under licensing or quota arrangements being consumer goods) and the Benelux list remaining the same.

The position in 1969 was as shown in *Table 4.1.*

It is Community practice that where particular commodities have been liberalised by the member-states they are added to a Community list. Once on this list a commodity cannot again be subject to a quota imposed by a member-state without Community authority. Possibly as a result of the Soviet–German trade treaty concluded in 1972 the number of items on the common liberalisation list has recently risen from 614 to 797.

Chapter 3 of the Treaty of Rome, which is concerned with Commercial Policy, lays down that the Commission will, after the end of the transitional period, conduct negotiations for agreements with third countries assisted by a special Committee appointed by the Council.

Table 4.1   LIBERALISATION OF EEC IMPORTS FROM COMECON COUNTRIES

Customs tariff headings	West Germany	France	Italy	Benelux
Completely liberalised	567	901	747	979
Partially liberalised	285	75	120	96
Not liberalised	245	121	230	22

Source: Third General Report on the Activities of the Communities, 1969.

Under Article 114 the agreements will be concluded by the Council on behalf of the Community. The requirement for a common external commercial policy for a grouping of states with separate Foreign Offices, balances of payments, and monetary authorities and with diverse traditions in the choice of trading partners, is extremely difficult to fulfil. The policy of the USSR and the East European states has contributed to the difficulties. By refusing to grant recognition to the EEC as a juridical unity and by largely boycotting the Commission they have impeded the growth of its authority in the field of East –West trade. But if during the transition period the member-states had felt it necessary either on political or economic grounds to implement the Treaty in this respect and act in common in their relations with the USSR and Eastern Europe they could have done so whether the USSR liked it or not. It is a reflection of the actual assessment of the *need* to act in common by the member-states that in this field common policy is still ineffective and even the completion of common procedures has been subject to endless delays.

As seen from the USSR the purpose of an EEC common policy is that 'the EEC countries will act in a single front in economic relations with the socialist countries while the latter are to act each in isolation'. As seen from Brussels the purpose of a common commercial policy is primarily internal. The starting point of serious discussion is to be found in a Commission memorandum dated 24 October 1962 which set out a programme of action for the second stage of the transitional period.

Between 1962 and 1964 the Commission made strenuous efforts to secure action on this programme, in particular by a memorandum of 26

February 1964 on the need to accelerate the establishment of a common commercial policy towards the state trading countries. The Commission's case for acceleration rested upon five propositions. The first, and probably the most important, was that the lack of harmonisation of commercial policies was having undesirable effects upon the Community's internal market. Secondly, since trade with Eastern Europe was becoming more and more important in GATT the Community must take up a common position in international negotiations. Thirdly, the Commission argued that the current (1964) fall in the Community's exports to Eastern Europe was due, apart from structural causes, to East European anticipation of the coming of a common policy. Fourthly, the Commission feared that in default of a new decision by the Council in this field the objectives defined by the Treaty for the end of the transitional period could not be guaranteed. Lastly, the Commission argued that as a uniform policy must cover all trade it was inconsistent to maintain a Community regime for agriculture and to leave trade in all other commodities to be regulated by national policies: under these conditions the negotiation of bilateral trade agreements would be unnecessarily difficult.

The Commission recognised that, because of its explosive political character, this question needed very cautious treatment in the Community. In the document of 26 February 1964 therefore it did not recommend an immediate transition to a common commercial policy but limited itself to presenting a programme for the gradual unification of the commercial policies of the member states. On 3 March 1964 the Council was asked to lay down a timetable for the stage-by-stage unification of policy towards the state trading countries by the end of the transitional period. It was hoped that it would be possible to conclude long-term agreements with the state trading countries as from the beginning of 1968. At the same time the Commission asked the Council to specify the main lines of future common *policy* towards the state trading countries, a request which has remained unanswered.

In January 1968 a report on the negotiation of agreements was referred to the experts of the member-states and on 26 February 1969 the Commission submitted to the Council a proposal for the unification of such agreements. When the Council examined this proposal it became clear that it was insufficient to cover all the problems arising from relations with third countries and the member-states insisted, in the interests of continuing trade relations, that in exceptional cases and for a limited period they should retain the right to negotiate their own commercial treaties. The Council discussions of 23 July and 15 September 1969 were decisive on this issue. As a result the Commission was forced to accept the existence of such 'special cases' but held that they could only be recognised where the application of Article 113 was prevented by circumstances beyond the control of the Community. The Commission decided to modify its February proposals and to provide for the 'exceptional' cases. It submitted a revised set of proposals to the Council on 8 October 1969, which conceded that during the period ending 31 December 1972 member-states may conclude bilateral agreements with third countries if, after discussion in a newly constituted Consultative Committee composed of representatives of the member-states under the Chairmanship of a member of the Commission, it is established that (a) negotiations under Article 113 are precluded for reasons beyond the control of the Community and (b) commercial relations with third countries are likely to be interrupted to the detriment of the Community if such bilateral agreements are not concluded.

In 'normal' cases, i.e. those which cannot be shown to be 'exceptional', the procedure established in the Commission's proposals was straightforward. For the prorogation or renewal of agreements already in force the member-state is to inform the Commission, three months in advance, that a treaty is due for prorogation or renewal. It is then discussed in the Consultative Committee, which takes into consideration the treaties between other member-states and the third country concerned. If the proposals for prorogation or renewal pass this scrutiny the Commission may propose to the Council that the member-state or states prorogue or renew the treaty for one year, or if it contains the 'EEC clause' or an annual denunciation clause it may be renewed for a longer period. The Commission may report to the Council if in the course of the consultation it appears that the treaty imperils a common commercial policy because of the disparities between the policies of the member-states.

For the negotiation of new agreements the procedure established was that a member-state may inform the Commission and other member-states that a treaty should be negotiated. The suggestion is then examined by the Consultative Committee which considers it in the light of Article 113 of the Treaty of Rome and decides whether the conditions for the opening of negotiations are present. If the proposal passes this scrutiny the Commission conducts the negotiation in consultation with a special committee composed of representatives of the member-states. These proposals were adopted by the Council of Ministers in December 1969. The summit meeting of the nine members of the enlarged Community declared its intention of pursuing a common commercial policy towards Eastern Europe as from 1 January 1973.

In fact, although the procedures are intended to come into effect at the beginning of 1973 there will be no reason to invoke them on a major scale until 1975, since France and Italy have recently negotiated agreements with the USSR and most East European states which run to

47

the end of 1974. Britain's existing agreements expire at the same time and a long-term agreement on trade and economic co-operation between the Federal Republic of Germany and the USSR was initialled in Moscow on 7 April 1972 and signed on 6 July 1972. The two parties agreed to provide favourable conditions for the development of trade, for improving the structure of trade turnover and for widening economic co-operation between organisations and firms of both states. The co-operation will include the building of industrial projects and the exchange of patents and licences. A mixed Soviet–German Commission to monitor and develop this co-operation was established and held its first meeting in Bonn on 19 April with Dr. Schiller, the Federal Minister of Economics and Finance in the chair.

In common with most West European countries the general EEC 'attitude' (as represented both by the governments of the member-states and by the decisions of the Community institutions) towards Eastern Europe has changed over the past seven or eight years. If we take a report prepared by M. Löhr under the auspices of the Commission in April 1965 as typical of the period we find the attitude to be on the whole defensive. The fear of East European 'dumping' is present. There is anxiety about the political orientation of Communist trade and the danger to Western countries implicit in becoming too dependent on Eastern Europe. The EEC must present a united front to defend itself: the volume of credit must be limited.

In March 1968 a report prepared by M. Hahn submitted resolutions to the vote of the Assembly (European Parliament), on the one hand urging the completion of the EEC commercial policy, open access to EEC markets for East European agricultural products and a common credit policy, and on the other stressing the importance of East–West trade in Europe, welcoming the signs of multilateralism in Eastern Europe and the appearance of more flexible market policies there, and looking forward to the unfreezing of 'blocs' and a closer interpenetration of the two parts of the Continent in commercial, technological and political co-operation as objectives through which the division of Europe may be overcome. In the Assembly debate on the report M. Jean-François Deniau, a member of the Commission, was considerably more cautious than Hahn in advocating liberal relations with Eastern Europe, but he accepted that a united Community should move into a phase of active trade expansion with Eastern Europe.

The same general attitude is to be found in a statement made on behalf of the EEC to the 26th Session of the ECE in the spring of 1971, which asserted that East–West trade is at a turning point, that it is capable of vast development and that a good atmosphere prevails in economic relations between all the countries of Europe.

The EEC's commercial agreement with Yugoslavia in 1970 stimulated a substantial growth of trade between that country and the EEC member-states. In 1972, 57% of Yugoslavia's trade was with the EEC member-states as against .30% with the Comecon member-states. The EEC has said that this situation should be helped in the future by the application of the generalised preference system—a system for giving preference to developing countries agreed upon at the United Nations Conference on Trade and Development (UNCTAD) at its second meeting in Delhi—to Yugoslavia. The Commission, in its report on the activities of the Communities in 1971, said that the economic opportunities (i.e. preferences) offered to the Third World can also apply to the Socialist countries. It is for a preferential argument of this kind that Rumania is negotiating.

In the field of economics—itself powerfully influenced by a changing political environment—it is reasonable to hope for the maintenance of a positive EEC attitude towards relations with Eastern Europe. The slow process of establishing policies and procedures need not have adverse effects upon that attitude. The brief historical sketch given in this chapter of the attempt to establish such policies and procedures shows that for the most part they were not directed against Eastern Europe, that where in the earlier days of the EEC a defensive attitude did underlie some of the attempts to find a policy that attitude has been substantially modified, and that the frustration of the attempts has been due partly to differences between the interests of the member-states and partly to a lack of any sense of urgency in devising means of confronting Eastern Europe on a unitary community basis. It is evident that the majority of the member-states were not convinced that solid commercial advantages could be gained by hastening the establishment even of common procedures in dealing with Eastern Europe: otherwise the course of events would have been different. The purely economic arguments in favour of a co-ordinated policy towards Eastern Europe have been comparatively weak and really cogent only when they were directed to the adverse *internal* effects of the lack of such a policy. And it is to be noted that it is *policy* which matters. Procedures required under the Treaty may well be more rapidly implemented in the latter half of the 1970s than they were between 1958 and 1972, but procedures without policy make little difference to conduct. On the other hand 'policy' itself is a question-begging word. It suggests firmness, a long-term view, clear objectives, planning. But so long as the decision-maker is conscious of the nature of his conduct and of the results it produces and is not merely carried along in a state of ignorance by events, 'policy' can equally well be flexible, expedient and pragmatic. By one means or another the decision-making process within the EEC has so far produced a minimum community policy towards Eastern Europe in economic affairs, the member-states (who after all compose the Council of Ministers, the supreme decision-making body) preferring to leave the major part of the conduct of East–West relations in their own hands. However arrived at, this *is* a policy, representing a particular balance between the requirements of the Treaty, the internal coherence of the Common Market and the possibilities of economic relations with Eastern Europe. There is a general agreement that economic relations with Eastern Europe should be expanded (and upon this issue there is no disagreement between the Commission and the member-states). This, however arrived at, is also a policy.

The most important change of policy which could occur would be a decision to give the economic and political coherence of the enlarged Community a much greater weight in the threefold balance between Treaty requirements, internal market conditions and external economic relations. The common negotiation of trade agreements is not necessarily a change of *policy* in this sense; it may equally well be treated as a procedural device to which the member-states have committed themselves by signing the Treaty. Unless in the meantime the member-states of the enlarged Communities decide that an entirely new type of economic relationship with Eastern Europe is required or unless a major step towards economic union (such as monetary unification) is taken which automatically limits the member-states' freedom of action the adoption of the procedure is likely to leave the initiative with the member-states and keep the 'corrective' actions of the Community institutions to a minimum.

The establishment of a full common economic policy towards Eastern Europe is therefore likely to be a consequence either of internal developments which make the pursuit of a common external economic policy inevitable or perhaps of an independent move towards political unification of the Nine for which the unification of external economic policy would serve as the instrument or symbol.

5 West European integration and economic relations with Eastern Europe, 1958–1969

There is general agreement among the countries of Western and Eastern Europe that trade between them should be increased and economic relations in general improved. In fact trade between the countries of Western and Eastern Europe has been growing rapidly over the past decade and a half although it still forms a comparatively small proportion of the total trade of most of the countries involved. That it has grown in this way is a sign that some of the prejudices which once operated have been to some extent overcome.

Both sides entered a new phase in the 1950s after the death of Stalin and the ending of the Korean War, but with strongly 'defensive' attitudes of mind in regard to their economic relations with each other. Neither was prepared to see its trade exchanges with the other grow to such a magnitude that the fortunes of its own economy became dependent on the other. Both harboured the suspicion that trade could be so handled as to promote political aims, in particular to detach groups or even nations from their political alliances. In addition, Western and Eastern European states had special fears arising from the nature of their economic systems. To Western states it seemed all too probable that the planned economies of the East, where costs and prices were related (if related at all) in a way incomprehensible to Western economists and businessmen, could use the powers of state foreign trade enterprises to sell at abnormally low prices and disrupt Western markets. To Eastern states the concept of an uncontrolled flow of commodities from outside the system into their domestic markets was totally alien to the principle of central economic planning. Whereas, at least in theory, Western states believed in the principles of a multilateral economy both among themselves and with the rest of the world, the Eastern states, which had adopted a method of balancing their economic relations with each other bilaterally and were therefore committed to applying the same principle with the countries of the West, believed that bilateralism was necessary to the maintenance of the planned economy. Lastly there were problems arising from the differences in the level of industrialisation in Western and Eastern Europe. It has been a major objective of Communist planning, since the first Soviet Five Year Plan was introduced in 1928, to hasten the progress of industrialisation and to bring it up to the level of the major Western states, both in terms of size and efficiency. Rapid though progress has been, equality has not yet been achieved; from the point of view of the present study the most important consequence is that Eastern Europe has an inadequate range of industrial products saleable in the West and has had to rely upon the export of foodstuffs and raw materials to pay for its imports of manufactured goods from the West, so establishing a relationship in foreign trade more akin to that of a developing region with a developed one than that of one developed region with another.

To meet these complex circumstances, some arising from political attitudes and some from differences in the economic systems but *none at all from the process of integration*, the EEC states in practice regulated their economic relations with the states of Eastern Europe during the transition phase 1958–1969 by bilateral arrangements of two main types which were also in use by other Western states outside the Community. Much the largest group of arrangements consisted in bilateral trade agreements, the other in agreements covering economic, industrial, scientific and technical co-operation.

The provisions of trade agreements differed from case to case, but most of those in force between the EEC states and the Comecon states contained two features in common. One was that for some commodities—varying from agreement to agreement—quotas were established, that is to say a maximum value was set for imports of those commodities in a given year. The second was a 'price clause' which provided that export prices should be those of the world market or those customary in the markets of the member-states. Taken together these provisions suggest that trade agreements are important regulators of the flow of commodities between the countries of Western and Eastern Europe. Certainly the East European states seem to value them for the part they can play in drawing up foreign trade plans, i.e. as an element of precision in forecasting.

Such agreements are however less important in practice as regulators of trade than they appear to be in principle. In the first place, the quantity of goods to be exchanged is in effect no more than a general indication of the level of trade to be aimed at: the agreement does not guarantee that the values will be reached and it is not a contract. Secondly, those parts of the agreements which specify actual quotas are by no means the whole: there will be a considerable range of commodities for which no quotas are fixed although the importer will need to obtain a licence to import. As the EEC member-states have 'liberalised' their imports from East Europe from quotas, as described in Chapter 4, so this quantitative element in trade agreements has declined. It will be seen from *Table 4.1* that even West Germany, the least 'liberal' (by this standard) of the EEC states, completely liberalised over half of the commodities formerly subject to quotas, whereas Benelux liberalised almost all commodities from quotas. Thirdly, it is not without significance that Western Germany, the EEC state with the largest overall exchange with Eastern Europe, was the least well-equipped with formal trade agreements until 1971, when a long-term agreement was reached with Czechoslovakia. A long-term agreement was initialled in April 1972 and signed in July of the same year. Until the negotiation of a new trade agreement with Poland began in 1970 West German trade with that country was governed by annual agreements. The large exchange between Western and Eastern Germany by a protocol of the Treaty of Rome is considered as 'internal' trade and is not covered by a trade agreement. The effect is that so long as this protocol remains in force, West German imports from Eastern Germany are not subject to the Common External Tariff of the EEC but are regulated by quantitative measures of which the West German government is required to keep the other EEC member-States informed. Trade agreements perform a politico-economic rather than a purely economic function: apart from the fact that they contain a goodwill clause pledging the contracting parties to do all in their power to encourage reciprocal trade exchanges and to maintain their stability, they also provide for mixed commissions of the contracting states to supervise the implementation of the agreement and to establish annual quota lists. The Soviet–German agreement of 1972, as we have already seen in the preceding chapter, 1972 provides for the establishment of such a Commission. To this extent trade agreements formalise and confirm the bilateral pattern of trade relations. Since the end of the transition period France has concluded long-term trade agreements (1970–1974) with Bulgaria, East Germany, Hungary, Poland, Rumania and the USSR; Italy with East Germany, Poland, Czechoslovakia, Hungary and the USSR.

As a possible pointer to the future it is of interest that Denmark which is now anew member of the EEC, recently concluded a trade agreement with the USSR which contains no quota lists: instead it simply sets out the intention to expand mutual trade. The UK itself practises the system of 'open' general or individual licensing which reduces the importance of quotas in trade agreements with Eastern Europe and in recent years has been rapidly liberalising its remaining quota lists.

The second main type of agreement is that relating to co-operation between Western and Eastern governments. These are essentially political documents demonstrating that the signatories favour the development of long-term economic ties and in so doing of course indicate to individual enterprises that they will have governmental support in their own efforts to co-operate. Such agreements may either be drawn up independently of trade agreements, or included as letters or annexes to trade agreements. More recently they have been combined with trade agreements in a single document. The Soviet–German agreement of 1972 appears to be an agreement of this comprehensive type. The first co-operation agreement was drawn up between Benelux and Poland in 1965, the latest was the long-term (10 years) economic agreement between France and the USSR drawn up in October 1971.

The co-operation agreements do not usually set out precise obligations, define 'co-operation' or restrict it to a particular sphere of activity. Their special importance in the field of East–West relations is twofold. In the first place they are long-term bilateral arrangements between *states* and in all cases provide that a 'Mixed Commission' of representatives of the two states shall be set up to supervise their implementation: for example, France, the UK and Western Germany all have such 'Mixed Commissions' with the USSR. In these circumstances the role of EEC 'community institutions' in industrial co-operation is at present limited. In the second place the practical co-operation that flows from them is between 'enterprises' on each side, between producer-units in the same field of production. The significance of this is that Western and Eastern economies become 'engaged' at a level below not only that of the integrated group but of the national state also. Agreements at enterprise level are not wholly dependent upon governmental agreements.

The originators of inter-enterprise co-operation were Austria and Western Germany, Poland and Hungary in the late 1950s. The practice subsequently spread to all the countries of Eastern Europe (except Albania) and many market economies in Europe, North America and Japan. A survey by the Secretariat of the United Nations Conference on Trade and Development in June 1969 listed 122 agreements made at the enterprise level of which 25 involved the UK, 25 West Germany, 16 France, 14 Austria, 11 Sweden and 9 Italy. The EEC countries between them accounted for a total of 54, somewhat less than half the European total. Since 1969 the numbers have grown substantially. The Treaty of Rome makes no reference to co-operation agreements and does not make any formal provision for bringing them under the control of Community institutions.

Integration in Western Europe has so far had little effect upon the methods by which the member-states of EEC or EFTA and the industrial and commercial enterprises based within them arrange their affairs in trade and co-operation with partners in Eastern Europe. Neither the EEC nor EFTA has engaged in state-trading: they are not themselves buyers or sellers of commodities. Nor for the most part do the governments of the member-states undertake actual market transactions. The role both of the state and of the integrated group (in so far as it has yet established one) has been to influence the environment within which private enterprises and corporations can operate. It is the enterprise which undertakes *transactions*.

In Eastern Europe until quite recently the enterprise has had an almost negligible role in external economic relations. Until the late 1960s each state drew up a comprehensive foreign trade and foreign exchange plan and the foreign transactions arising from the plan were exclusively in the hands of foreign trade corporations responsible for exporting or importing particular classes of commodity. Taut foreign trade planning of this kind was well equipped to live with bilaterally negotiated levels of trade, with trade agreements, quotas and all other forms of quantitative regulation. Above all it was well suited to a philosophy of foreign trade based upon the planning of imports to make good gaps in the domestic economic plan. All East European currencies were (and still are) inconvertible which meant that foreigners could not hold balances of the currency of a particular country and use them for the purchase either of other currencies or of the goods produced in that country. From this it followed that trade accounts were balanced bilaterally between the East European states themselves. Western currencies became convertible for East–West trade purposes in the 1950s and therefore could be used for the settlement of accounts between Eastern and Western countries; but before an Eastern country could plan its imports from a Western country it had to be reasonably sure that it had enough Western currencies in hand to settle the bill, or good prospects of credit from its Western partners. Exports were thought of primarily as the means of procuring the Western currencies necessary to pay for the imports required for the domestic plan.

Under this 'import-orientated' East European system the East European import plans were perhaps the most important single determinant of the level of East–West trade in Europe. Firms in West European states could not greatly affect the level of trade by launching exports at the East European states in excess of their import plans. Conversely the East European countries were unlikely to engage in *major* export drives in excess of the foreign trade plan merely to secure reserves of convertible currencies. Only a change in the foreign trade plan could motivate export efforts. Under such a system the producer-enterprise could be granted very little, if any, scope for initiative in the field of foreign trade.

The beginnings of change in this foreign trade system coincided with the period of general reform of the planning system of the East European states which began, in East Germany, in 1963, and reached its most advanced form in Hungary in 1968. The role of trade in determining the size of the national income, the allocation of resources and the general management of the economy played a part in the discussion of reform (except in the USSR) and the reforms themselves introduced new features into the conduct of foreign trade. Perhaps the most significant was the adoption of a new attitude towards exports as such. In all the East European states various forms of export incentives were introduced. But if exports are to become a *leading* rather than a *secondary* factor in determining the state's balance of payments, the producer-enterprise must be given much greater freedom to operate in Western markets. No foreign trade corporation can *plan* exports *in general*, more particularly if the purpose is to obtain an export surplus. The state trading system by dint of hard bargaining may, indeed must, somehow provide exports to match imports and bring the two into balance, but to go beyond this and earn foreign currency 'in advance', as it were, means that the producer must launch into the unknown, operate like any other enterprise in Western markets and persuade customers to buy. As a consequence of the reforms in Eastern Europe there has been some reduction (varying from country to country) in the rigour of the import plan so that for example in Hungary enterprises can draw credits from the banks to purchase a considerable range of foreign goods on their own initiative. Further, branch industrial associations and enterprises have acquired the right to undertake transactions in foreign markets. These changes have gone furthest in Bulgaria, Rumania, and Hungary but it seems likely that Poland will also adopt a more flexible system in the near future. No changes have occurred in the Russian system, nor are any likely to occur in the foreseeable future.

In the field of *trade* three trends are observable over the past 5–6 years: (a) some 'liberation' of East European imports from the rigours of total planning, (b) a tendency for East European economies to be more export-orientated, and, consequently, (c) an increase in the active involvement of enterprises in foreign trade transactions. This third, and highly important, development has been reinforced by the extension of industrial *co-operation* between Western and Eastern enterprises, which involve the participants in a degree of integration of their manufacturing cycles.

It would be unwise to assume that these changes in East Europe imply a radical or universal change in the system. They are still comparatively experimental and need to prove their worth in terms of improved balances of payments with Western countries. They are too recent and too limited in scope to have had any significant effect upon the trading situation as between Western and Eastern Europe as yet.

It will be seen that between 1958 and 1969 the conditions under which trade between Western and Eastern Europe was transacted were slowly changing as diverse factors affected the bilateral relations between the states—on the one hand the development of economic integration in the form of the customs union and the common agricultural policy of the EEC, the free trade area within EFTA in Western Europe and the planning of trade within Comecon; on the other a more positive attitude to East–West trade in both Western and Eastern Europe and the development of more liberal, or less restrictive, methods of state control over the flow of commodities. The systems themselves did not change significantly; Western Europe was still operating on the principles of the 'market economy', Eastern Europe on the principles of central economic planning. Neither the EEC nor Comecon as institutions played a significant part in controlling the trade flows. So diverse are these factors in the situation that it is impossible to estimate what total effect they had upon the actual development of trade.

The table in Appendix I (p. 101) sets out in a simple form the growth of 'total' trade (the value of exports of West European countries to the Comecon states plus a) Western the value of exports of the Comecon states to West European states) between Western Europe as a whole, (b) EEC and (c) EFTA and their trading partners in Comecon. In value terms all three sets of trade figures show a striking increase between 1958 and 1971, all three showing considerable fluctuations in rates of growth as between one year and another. Over the period the share of the EEC generally increased, while that of EFTA, after rising substantially between 1961 and 1964 and subsequently declining, was comparatively stable. The two 'integrated' organisations in Western Europe were between them tending to absorb a larger slice of total trade between Western and Eastern Europe at the expense of the 'rest' of Western Europe towards the end of the period.

The discussion in the three preceding chapters will of course have made it clear that the totals shown in the Appendix table for the exchanges between Western Europe, EEC and EFTA and the Comecon states are arithmetical only; they are the sum of exchanges between the individual states forming the various groups and do not represent exchanges managed by the groups as units. On both sides the individual nation states have had diverse experiences in the level and rate of growth of trade with their partners and in the resulting trade balances.

The enlargement of the EEC share of the total does not necessarily indicate that the form of organisation adopted by the Common Market is 'superior', in this context, to that of EFTA. In theory perhaps the customs union plus other forms of harmonisation within the Common

Market should give the member-states a competitive advantage over the looser free-trade area system of EFTA, but it cannot be satisfactorily demonstrated that this alone accounted for the somewhat better EEC performance; other factors such as the energy displayed by West Germany, France and Italy in developing the East European market played a major part, which cannot be quantified. It will be noticed too that the year in which the EEC–Comecon showed the highest growth rate was 1960, before the customs union was complete and that this sector suffered a much severer set-back between 1961 and 1964 than any other. What can be said however is that the degree of integration achieved by the EEC in its 'transitional phase' up to 1969 was not incompatible with a higher rate of growth and an expanding share in East–West trade in Europe. On this evidence alone the enlargement of the Community should not prove harmful to the growth of East–West trade.

One of the most significant features of the table is the fall in the trade growth-rate between 1961 and 1964 and its revival after 1965. The recession of 1961–1964 was largely due to the development of adverse East European balances of payments, leading to serious shortages in their holdings of Western currencies. The restoration of the generally strong growth rate after 1965 was in large part due to the policy of 'liberalising' imports on the part of the Western states (including those of the EEC) and of increasing the supply of Western credits to East European borrowers. Thus the principal effect of liberalisation was to restore a situation which threatened to deteriorate, rather than to initiate an entirely new period of expansion. That Western Europe and the EEC in particular has already 'used up' a significant part of the liberalisation measures available to it without producing an exceptionally rapid increase in the growth-rate of trade since 1965 is one reason for caution in speculating about the future growth of trade.

If we now turn to consider the balance of trade (i.e. the difference between the value of imports and exports) the difference between EEC and EFTA experience is more marked.

Until 1967 the value of EEC's imports from the Comecon states as a whole exceeded the value of its exports, i.e. there was an overall deficit. But this overall deficit was made up of two parts—a general *surplus* with the non-Russian member-states, more than offset by a large and continuing deficit with the USSR. In 1967 for the first time the EEC moved into surplus with Comecon. In 1969 the balance of EEC trade with the USSR itself also moved into surplus, unlike the balances between OECD as a whole and more particularly that of EFTA. On average, EFTA balances with the Comecon states as a whole were more persistently in deficit and to a much greater amount than those of the EEC. This deficit was especially pronounced in trade with the

USSR but applied to the non-Russian members also from time to time. The UK balance of trade with the USSR has been uniformly in deficit for many years. The effect was that throughout the 1960s the USSR in particular was earning far more Western currencies from EFTA than from the EEC and, since all West European currencies are convertible for East–West trade, the USSR, if it so chose, could spend a part of its surplus earnings from EFTA states upon purchases from the EEC. Until 1967 the non-Russian states of Comecon were also earning more Western currencies from their trade with EFTA than from their trade with EEC and could, if they chose, use this surplus to buy EEC goods. In 1967 the balance of trade between EFTA and the non-Russian states of Comecon moved into and remained in rough equilibrium. The enlargement of the Community by bringing in the UK, which had the largest and most persistent trade deficit with the USSR of all the EFTA states, may have the immediate effect of putting the EEC balance into deficit again, but since a considerable part of the USSR's earnings from member-states in deficit are likely to be spent within the EEC and since the UK on entering the EEC will begin to take steps to run down the sterling area, where in the past a substantial part of the USSR's earnings from the UK were spent, the EEC is likely to benefit in terms of its trade balance in the longer run. However, the course of trade with the USSR is subject to wide and unpredictable fluctuations and no confident forecast can be made.

The major part of the imports of Western Europe from Eastern Europe consists in food and raw materials: the major part of Western Europe's exports in manufactured products of all kinds, especially chemicals and machinery. In this, the 'composition' of their trade with Eastern Europe, EEC and EFTA are very much alike.

Of the EEC's imports from Eastern Europe two groups, foodstuffs and manufactures, are of special significance for the future. The first, foodstuffs, gradually came under the regulation of the Common Agricultural Policy during the period and its fortunes under the new system should give some pointer to the future especially when the agricultural imports of the new members of the Communities come under the same regulation. Table 5.1 shows the relationship between the EEC's total imports of foodstuffs from all sources (including Eastern Europe), at dates between 1958 and 1959 in millions of dollars and its imports from Eastern Europe.

The Common Agricultural Policy came into being in January 1962 and by July 1968 covered most agricultural products. The general principle of the policy is that agricultural imports should be free of quantitative restrictions but prices are kept above world levels by imposing levies at the frontiers of the Community so as to bring prices up to the 'target price' of the Community. The policy does not intentionally discriminate against any particular supplier although of course it operates to the disadvantage of suppliers capable of selling at

Table 5.1   EEC IMPORTS OF FOODSTUFFS

Year	(a) Total imports of foodstuffs	(b) Imports from Eastern Europe	(b) as % of (a)
1958	4 020	152	3·78
1960	5 475	233	4·25
1963	7 081	375	5·29
1966	9 346	536	5·6
1968	9 822	574	5·84
1969	11 491	622	5·5

Sources: EEC and UN statistics.

low prices. Most East European states insist that the CAP has harmed their trade in these products with the EEC. It may of course be the case that without the CAP the EEC's imports from Eastern Europe would have been greater than they were. This is impossible to prove or disprove. The table shows however that the proportion of the EEC's imports of food from *all* sources coming from Eastern Europe (although a small proportion of the whole) (*a*) was bigger in 1969 than in 1958 or 1960, (*b*) did not decrease after the coming into force of the CAP.

In 1969 the UK's total imports of foodstuffs from all sources amounted to $4 642 m. Of this total, $166 m came from Eastern Europe. The Eastern Europe share in the UK's total imports was therefore 3·6%—somewhat below that of the EEC of the Six.

The second group of imports—manufactures—is important for a number of reasons. In the first place in the modern world trade between industrialised regions is largely in manufactured products, often reflecting differences in preference for different qualities and prices of the same product (e.g. between cars, machinery, textiles, radio sets) as between consumers in different countries. If the sophistication of tastes and discrimination between prices and qualities in products were to be removed the level of trade between the advanced regions would be

considerably reduced. To enter effectively into this type of international exchange therefore Eastern Europe needs to allow for, and to respond to, the sense of discrimination among its own consumers, and to initiate products which will appeal to the tastes (as regards quality and price) of buyers in other industrialised regions. Without this,

Eastern Europe as an industrialising region cannot share in the characteristic exchanges of the advanced countries and the general growth of trade with those states will be inhibited. In the second place the existing hard currency-earning non-industrial exports from Eastern Europe to Western Europe are vulnerable. In certain respects Comecon as a whole is short of many basic materials for its own use and internal consumption is bound to rise. In the longer term therefore the supply of such materials to the world market may be reduced because of increasing domestic demand. The same consideration applies to foodstuffs: rising standards of life within Comecon will inevitably create a greater internal demand (as they have done in the EEC) for varied foodstuffs with high protein and vitamin content, such as meat, fish, dairy produce, vegetables and fruit. Agricultural production is notoriously a problem sector in the East European economies and in Western Europe is subject to a wide variety of protective measures for social and political reasons.

Throughout the period 1958–1969 the proportion of manufactures in the total of West European imports from Eastern Europe remained almost static. For the period 1957–1959 engineering goods accounted for 9·9% of Western Europe's imports from Eastern Europe: in the period 66–1968 for 0·4%. For other manufactures in the same two periods the percentages were 9·7 and 10·6. The Economic Commission for Europe has concluded that in terms of constant prices the broad commodity structure of East European exports to Western Europe probably remained unchanged over the period 1957–1968. But the commodity composition of West Europe's imports from *all* sources changed very considerably during the period, the share of manufactures increasing from 34% to 48%. In respect of this group of commodities the position of East European manufactures in West European markets in relation to West European imports from the rest of the world actually deteriorated. On the other hand it is clear that manufactures as a proportion of East Europe's exports to the world as a whole did not greatly increase during the period. In 1960 26·5% of East Europe's total exports to the world consisted of machinery: in 1969 the share had risen to 30·6%. In 1960 manufactured consumer's goods accounted for 8·9% of total East European exports: in 1969 they accounted for 9·0%. It will be seen therefore that Eastern Europe had not been very successful in expanding this sector of its export pattern in the world market.

The pattern of East European trade with the EEC does not differ significantly from that of Western Europe as a whole. In 1958 12% of the EEC's imports from Eastern Europe consisted of manufactures (i.e. finished products such as leather goods, paper, fabrics, glass, chemicals, machinery, transport equipment, instruments and consumer goods), in

1960 15%, in 1963 10%, in 1966 14%, in 1969 17%. As between the beginning and end of the period there is a general tendency for the share to increase: a tendency which became more marked in the last 3–4 years but a radical change in the trade pattern will take many years to accomplish.

The growth in, and slow diversification of trade between, Western and Eastern Europe has hitherto been a comparatively sheltered section of world trade. The USA has not seriously entered as a competitor of Western Europe in East European markets and it was only towards the end of the period that Japan began to be a major competitor in both Western and Eastern European markets.

As a result of the Soviet-American 'Summit' meeting in May 1972 trade and other forms of economic co-operation between the two countries, for so long in the doldrums, will now expand. Japanese trading and technical arrangements with the USSR and Eastern Europe are also growing in number and value. Both are technologically advanced countries with much to offer Eastern Europe. Their entry into East –West trade and co-operation may considerably disturb the hitherto predominantly European character of these exchanges and possibly restrict the future rate of growth of the European Sector.

6 An enlarged EEC and the prospects for East–West economic relations in Europe

The trade of the enlarged EEC with Eastern Europe will encompass a very substantial share of the total of East–West trade in Europe. The effect of enlargement is shown in *Table 6.1*.

Table 6.1 THE EFFECT OF ENLARGEMENT ON THE EEC'S SHARE OF EAST–WEST IN EUROPE*

	EEC of Six	EEC of Nine
	Percentage Share of West European total	*Percentage Share of West European total*
Exports of all Commodities to Eastern Europe	51·5	63·8
Exports of agricultural products	34·7	42·6
Exports of raw materials	46·0	59·6
Exports of manufactures	58·0	67·2
Imports of all commodities from Eastern Europe	46·1	64·4
Imports of agricultural products	63·4	80·4
Imports of raw materials	43·7	66·1
Imports of manufactures	35·8	51·8

*Based upon 1969 trade returns.
Source: United Nations Economic Bulletin for Europe, Vol. 22, No. 1, Tables B and C.

The increased EEC share is mainly due to the inclusion of Britain, one of the most important of Eastern Europe's trading partners in Western Europe. In 1969 the EEC of the Six exported $1952·8 million of manufactured goods to Eastern Europe. Britain exported $404·5 million. In both cases the principal item was machinery. The EEC imported $702·1 million of agricultural products, Britain $166·4 million: the EEC imported $1231·5 million of raw materials and semi-manufactures, Britain $536 million.

The most important *immediate* consequence of the enlargement of the EEC will be to subject over 80% of West Europe's imports of agricultural products (almost all being foodstuffs) to the Common Agricultural Policy of the EEC. Since raw materials are subject to low or zero tariffs in both the EEC and Britain, British entry will make little difference to the situation which existed before enlargement. Moreover the importation of raw materials into Britain is almost free of quotas (98% of British imports from the USSR are quota-free). The Common External Tariff of the EEC, which Britain and the other applicants will accept on joining, principally affects the importation of manufactured goods, but the differences between British tariffs and the Common External Tariff are not great enough for the harmonisation of the two to have a major effect upon the competitiveness of East European imports of this class in the enlarged Community. Agricultural imports from Eastern Europe, which as we saw in the previous chapter are a major balancing item in East–West trade, are those most likely to be adversely affected by the enlargement of the EEC, the consequences being felt unequally by the East European states: Poland, which supplies large quantities to the British market, being the most vulnerable, the USSR, from which Britain buys raw materials but little foodstuffs, the least vulnerable. The Common Agricultural Policy will be the principal focus of controversy, and most probably of negotiation, for the enlarged EEC.

The enlargement of the EEC's share of Western Europe's commodity trade with Eastern Europe suggests a very considerable enhancement of the EEC's 'power' in its relations with Eastern Europe. But this notion needs to be treated with great care. The group has a gross national product nearly two-thirds the size of the American and more than twice as large as that of the Soviet Union. Its population is larger than that of the USA or the USSR. Considered as a unit it is the largest trading group in the world. Its gold reserves match those of the USA and its combined vote in the International Monetary Fund is larger than the American. These are impressive indications of 'strength' in statistical terms; but of course strength is not merely a matter of size: it is equally a matter of the co-ordinated use of resources. Unless the levels of EEC trade are centrally controlled and can be freely adjusted to respond to 'tough' or 'soft' policies by the Community acting as a unit, the sheer size of the trading figures has very little to do with power relationships. 'Power' in this context means the ability and willingness to concede or deny benefits to the negotiating partner in the interests of a generalised common policy—which might or might not be purely economic. The EEC as it is today or as it is likely to be for many years to come is not so integrated or so centralised that it could, as a unit, disregard the interests of the member-states or the enterprises operating within them in pursuance of a power game played with trading counters.

The scale of the trading relations between the EEC and Comecon by no means implies that they are in a position to act as monopolists towards each other. An integrated group of states with a common external policy will only be able to attempt monopolist behaviour in sales if a very large proportion of the supply of particular commodities originates within the group and if all the producers within the group are either integrated into one enterprise or form an exclusive cartel, acting under instructions from the community institutions. Now the contemporary process of concentration in particular industries within the EEC does not take place exclusively between the enterprises of the Nine. Mergers and multinational companies often involve other enterprises, especially American, outside the Communities, so that over a wide range of commodities if a 'monopolistic' position were within the bounds of possibility it would only rarely be coterminous with the boundaries of the Common Market. In practice however the establishment of a monopoly in the types of product traded between the EEC and Comecon states would rarely be possible even for a short period.

Theoretically, the EEC could more easily approach a position of monopsonist as buyer, because the single commercial policy of a very large integrated market can be used to affect the volume and prices of imports. The central administration of tariff levels, quantitative restrictions and monetary policies could be used to present a common bargaining position to Eastern Europe. But, given the nature of the commercial relations between Western and Eastern Europe as they now are, and as they are likely to remain for a foreseeable future, the exercise of monopsonistic power by the Community acting as a group would make very little sense. What would the EEC acting as a monopsonist hope to achieve? It is hardly likely to use its bargaining position to force *down* the prices of East European exports, since the principal fear in the past has been that these prices may already be unrealistically low. It could, theoretically, use monopsonistic power to discriminate between East European suppliers with the object of tying in one or more East European states more closely than others to its own market. But this would rightly be recognised by the East European states as politically motivated, and would provoke counter-action. Above all, with the existing structure of trade, reduction in the price-levels of imports from East Europe would inevitably and automatically reduce East European demand for EEC exports.

The use of monopsonistic power would be counter-productive.

A totally integrated Comecon, if the broad principles of foreign trade management were to remain unchanged, would operate a single import and foreign currency plan. Provided that the world demand situation for particular commodities is favourable, i.e. that a unitary Comecon is the dominant buyer of one or more commodities, it could be *administratively* equipped to act as a monopsonist for those commodities on the world market. In practice, although a unitary Comecon might be in a position to discriminate between different groups of world suppliers, e.g. by tying in a group of developing countries to its own import plans, it could not, because of the world supply situation, act as a monopsonist in relation to the EEC or Western Europe.

It cannot be assumed *a priori* that the characteristic developments of East–West economic relations in Europe between 1958 and 1969—rapid, if fluctuating, annual growth; some liberalisation of import controls, a flow of Western credits to sustain Western export surpluses, greater multilateralism in the payments system and growing industrial co-operation—will necessarily continue unchanged in the remaining decades of this century.

Apart from new factors such as the increase of Japanese competition in both West and East European markets and the imminent entry of the USA on a serious scale into trade with Eastern Europe, the most important long-term factor which could inhibit growth is the extremely slow rate of change in the commodity composition of East–West trade in Europe. The growth of exchanges between Western manufactures and East European foodstuffs and raw materials cannot continue to grow indefinitely. Projections recently made by the UN Economic Commission for Europe suggest that Western Europe's demand for agricultural products from Eastern Europe will not grow fast enough in the next ten years to make for a sharp increase in East Europe's share of Western Europe's imports: partly because East Europe's capacity to increase exports of livestock and meat is limited and because the East European domestic demand is likely to increase. The rising home demand for solid fuels and petroleum in Eastern Europe is likely to keep exports fairly stable although Soviet deliveries of gas may increase considerably. Western Europe is tending to substitute imports of end-products for the imports of crude materials. All in all the general prospects for the expansion of East European exports of food and raw materials to Western Europe are modest. Therefore in order to be able to purchase an increasing value of manufactures from Western Europe on the existing scale and to maintain the 1958–1969 rate of growth the East European countries must earn the requisite hard currency by selling more manufactures in Western Europe. The ECE estimates that East European exports of manufactures to Western Europe will need to grow by 15·2% by 1980 as compared with the 11·2% which was actually achieved between 1957 and 1967 to maintain an overall growth of 10% per annum. This would entail a relatively modest increase in East Europe's share of West European imports from 2·6% in 1965–1967 to 3·7% in 1980. Whether it can be achieved, or surpassed, will obviously depend above all on the ability of the East European states to develop types of commodities to meet West European tastes and the capacity to sell them.

What the EEC can itself do to stimulate this development is limited: the greater part of the initiative must come from the East European seller. The EEC as a member of GATT would find it virtually impossible to make unilateral discriminatory cuts *in favour* of Eastern Europe in its external tariff on East European manufactures and it seems likely that the EEC will be sparing in its grants of generalised preferences to East European states which feel they are qualified to receive them as 'developing' countries. In this respect the enlargement of the EEC will make little difference, since the commodity composition of the UK's trade with Eastern Europe is similar to that of the EEC and the new members will, on joining, be subject to the Common External Tariff. Much will depend on the value placed on the Eastern European market by West European, and especially EEC, manufacturing industry. If it is felt that this market must be expanded increasing pressure will be put upon governments and the Community institutions actively to encourage the import of East European manufactures. This would certainly be a matter for a common commercial policy in the EEC. Paradoxically, the enlargement of the EEC and the consolidation of its commercial policy, if East European manufacturers are capable of rising to the occasion, might actually help Eastern Europe over their hurdle.

If the 1958–1969 trends were to be continued unchanged until 1980, according to the ECE estimate, the West European export surplus would increase from less than $200 million in 1966–1968 to $3·5 billions in 1980. Such a gap would seem to be insupportable from the East European point of view. It must be covered by (*a*) the necessary increase in exports of manufactures to Western Europe, by (*b*) increased earnings of hard currency by sales elsewhere in the world, or (*c*) by Western credits. Western credits on this scale are unlikely to be acceptable to either side, but clearly the demand for them may rise well above existing levels and will require more exacting consideration by the EEC as a whole, within the framework of the general Western monetary system, than the present lower levels.

Industrial co-operation and joint ventures between Eastern and Western enterprises, although they have many merits, are unlikely to become a major substitute for traditional types of trade exchanges in the near future. In theory they could help to correct East Europe's adverse balance of payments (a) by eliminating the need for payment in foreign exchange between the co-operating enterprises and (b) by involving the Western partner in the sales of the joint product in hard currency areas, so making the Western partner responsible for promoting the exports of products which are in part East European. But Western enterprises are, naturally, cautious about undertaking excessive responsibilities for export promotion of this kind and the growth of co-operation is unlikely to become so rapid as to be able to eliminate more than a fraction of the East European adverse balance.

Nevertheless it is probably in the field of Western finance for, and technical participation in, the development of large capital projects in Eastern Europe, rather than in the field of 'conventional' trade that East–West economic relations will develop fastest. The new International Investment Bank of Comecon seems destined to play an important role in floating loans in Western European (and other) capital markets for this purpose. The capital needs of many East European states are so great that two of them, Hungary and Rumania, have gone so far as to authorise investment by foreigners in their enterprises. It seems highly probable that the big future developments in EEC /Comecon relations will not lie in niggling discussions about trading questions but in the field of inter-state (and later inter-community) technical and industrial agreements and in the world of international finance. Bankers will be at the centre of things.

The first signs of the major role which international financial operations seem destined to play in East–West economic relations have already appeared. In 1971 the National Bank of Hungary undertook a $25 million Eurobond flotation managed by the Moscow Narodny Bank and two London banks. This operation was followed in 1972 by heavy borrowing of convertible currencies by the International Bank for Economic Co-operation—the trading bank established by Comecon in 1964 to allow the member-states to settle their accounts with each other multilaterally in transferable roubles and intended also to act as a source of short and medium term credit (in which function it has not proved very successful). In February 1972 IBEC obtained a loan of $20 million arranged by a Franco-Belgian banking group, in March a loan of $60 million provided by French, German and Italian banks and in April a five-year loan of $60 million arranged by the Moscow Narodny and two other London banks and 16 other banks in Europe, North America and Japan. It will be noticed that the sources of these funds extend well beyond the boundaries of the EEC. The effect upon the convertible currency holdings of IBEC of this round of borrowing will be very striking, since the previous holdings of the bank probably stood at less than $20 million.

In principle it is unlikely that IBEC will use its new resources to support long-term investment in Comecon; the more probable use is for the financing of intra-Comecon trade and as a reserve which will enable the USSR to avoid the unpalatable use of the rouble in that role and also attract increasing business from the Comecon member-states. The International Investment Bank of Comecon, which came into operation at the beginning of 1971 and is charged with responsibility for providing long-term investment funds, has not yet fully shown its hand as an international borrower. Its statutes however empower it to raise loans in third countries so that, waiting in the wings, there is a Comecon financial institution, especially concerned with the technical progress and economic organisation which may well prove to be a much larger borrower on the international money markets than IBEC. The UK will take with her into the EEC the London money market, which is one of the most highly developed in the world for this type of international transaction.

Without labouring the point unduly we have to see the potentialities of the expansion of East–West trade and other economic relations in the new Europe which is to contain the enlarged Community in a sober light. The existing rate of expansion may indeed be maintained but there is no solid reason for supposing that it will grow astronomically. The new factors represented by industrial and financial co-operation cannot yet be fully assessed. It is against this background that we should consider how relations between an integrating Western Europe and an integrating Eastern Europe may be *conducted*.

If we extrapolate from the situation of the present and the immediate (12-year) past it is possible to separate out three distinct and possible competing tendencies: (*a*) the desire of Eastern Europe to give high priority to intra-Comecon trade and technological growth; (*b*) the desire of Eastern Europe, and especially the USSR, to *plan* economic relations between Western and Eastern Europe on a long-term basis; and (*c*) the preference of Western Europe, partially supported in Eastern Europe, to see East/West economic relations develop on a multilateral market basis.

It would seem, to judge from most recent Comecon pronouncements, including that of July 1971, that first priority is to be given in Eastern Europe to trade between the members of Comecon. Intra-Comecon trade already plays a major part in the external trade of most Comecon members (about 60% for USSR, 70% for East Germany, 60% for Poland, 65% for Czechoslovakia, 66% for Hungary, 50% for Rumania, 74% for Bulgaria, and in most cases the percentage increased between 1958 and 1969). An increase of this proportion would involve a further step towards self-sufficiency for the region. But full self-sufficiency is unlikely to be aimed at. In the first place so long as Western Europe, and other 'Western' states, are technological-ly more advanced than Eastern Europe, the Comecon states will wish to purchase their products. Secondly, it is an accepted Leninist princi-ple that trade with capitalist states is politically desirable. Thirdly, so long as the non-Russian states of Comecon can retain freedom to con-duct a significant part of their own external relations they can keep their own national lines to the West open. Fourthly, the Comecon states are concerned to expand their trading ralations with the develop-ing world. Fifthly, it is widely, though not universally, accepted in Eastern Europe that the advantages of international division of labour and specialisation may accrue not only from trade within Comecon but also from trade with the rest of the world. There are therefore limits to the policy of 'going it alone' on Comecon's part. If Eastern Europe does not 'go it alone' in relation to the rest of the world there is no reason why it should do so in relation to the EEC especially as the EEC states are, and will be to a greater extent after the enlargement of the Communities, a major supplier of advanced industrial equipment. The best hope perhaps is that increasing integration between producers in the Comecon states may within the next 10–15 years introduce econo-mies of scale and technical innovation sufficient to bring the quality and prices of East European manufactures to the levels expected in Western markets. If this does not happen closer integration and greater dependence on intra-Comecon trade could inhibit the growth of East –West economic relations.

Seen in this light the prevalent fear among East European states that the enlargement of the Community will damage their exports of food-stuffs to Western Europe is comparatively short-term. It is true that the enlargement of the Community will mean that about 80% of West Europe's food imports from Eastern Europe will be taken by the EEC, that these imports will be subject to the EEC's Common Agricultural Policy and that the UK will bring with it into the EEC transitional arrangements with New Zealand covering commodities of interest relations East European producers and that Ireland and Denmark are important agricultural producers. The short-term effect of enlargement is likely to be disadvantageous to East European agricultural exports; on the other hand enlargement could serve as an addi-tional stimulus to the diversification of the East European export pattern, which is the fundamental long-term requirement.

Given that economic relations between Eastern and ·Western Europe will develop at a moderate rather than dramatic rate of growth, that the Western system will be mainly market-orientated and the Eastern system mainly plan-orientated, and that each is engaged in the process of integration, how will ralations between them, and more particularly between the enlarged Community and the Comecon states, be conducted?

Relations between Eastern and Western partners are most likely to be *planned* in the field of large-scale capital projects. The construction of very large plants, especially those in the extractive industries which interest the USSR, is a long-term matter which may well require the commitment of consortia of Western industries and banks. Both sides in such types of undertaking require the guarantee of government backing, the signature of long-term contracts and assured methods of payments. As far as the enlarged Community is concerned firms from more than one member-state will almost certainly be involved. This kind of undertaking is an appropriate field for common policy in the EEC. In the first place the decision to enter upon such undertakings may have to be taken upon a Community basis. Secondly the provision and allocation of resources may well require close consultation between the states. Lastly it is a matter of policy to decide how big a part in the Community's economic relations with Eastern Europe massive long-term capital projects are to play.

Although state and 'community' intervention may be appropriate in the planning of major capital projects it is less appropriate to day-to-day *trading* transactions. At this level the most appropriate arrangement is for enterprises on both sides to do business with each other. Large-scale bilateralism between member-states and even more between the two integrated organisations as such will impede the operation of the principle of comparative advantage. Trade is more likely to be rational if it is the outcome of large numbers of separate transactions.

If they were to press for the extension of planning to East–West *trade* the East European states would in fact be pressing for a Western abandonment of liberal policies, since the only effective trade planning instruments available to Western states are precisely those forms of quantitative control, especially quota and licensing systems, which in the interests of liberalisation the Western states have been progressively giving up. From the Western point of view one cannot have liberality and trade planning at one and the same time. Now the EEC even if, or when, it is fully integrated is likely to adhere to a generally 'market' philosophy, i.e. while the member-states and community institutions concern themselves with the general trading environment actual market *transactions* remain in the hands of private or corporate enterprise. Integration of the EEC type does *not* imply that the Community becomes a buyer or seller in its own right. In Eastern Europe the enterprise at present is a very much less important factor in the field of foreign trade than the foreign trade monopoly but this is slowly changing. Faced with the urgent need to expand and diversify exports several East European states are giving greater freedom to enterprises to conduct foreign trade transactions. Furthermore the Comecon states have committed themselves in their pronouncement of July 1971 to creating the monetary conditions which will increase the scope of multilateral trade, at first within Comecon itself and later in relations with the West. An approach to a convertible rouble, to East European currency convertibility *vis-à-vis* the rouble, to single exchange rates and to more realistic foreign trade prices must have the effect of loosening tight planning control over the levels of foreign trade transactions and introducing additional market elements into the process.

The future development of East–West relations therefore places the long-standing debate between 'planning' and 'free enterprise' at the international level—the West preferring multilateral market operations and the East hoping for a high degree of planning. The most likely outcome is that in practice the European system will contain elements of both. And here it should be pointed out that planning does not necessarily mean that the community institutions of EEC and Comecon are involved in all operations. Long-term projects are equally possible between enterprises or between member-states. The role of Community institutions may perhaps in the large majority of cases be no more than that of providing a general framework. It is the *scale* of such operations more than anything else which will decide whether the Community institutions are involved; the larger the scale the more likely it is that Community institutions will be involved.

Extrapolation from the immediate past suggests that East–West economic relations in Europe will be of a 'mixed' type containing both planning and market elements. The enlargement of the Community of itself favours neither the one development nor the other. The much more important issue is whether the enlarged Community will pursue a single policy, or a 'group strategy' towards Eastern Europe and vice versa. The EEC is committed to the concept of a common external commercial policy; Comecon has included the concept in the programme published in 1971. If group strategies are eventually adopted will existing trends towards greater multilateralism in transactions be halted?

What gains would the enlarged EEC and Comecon hope to secure from pursuing group strategies or single policies?

Monetary unification, i.e. the creation of a single currency and a highly integrated banking system in both organisations, would actually *impose* group strategies under certain circumstances whether the organisations intend it or not, because with monetary unification the organisation becomes in certain respects equivalent to a very large single state in its external monetary relations, especially as regards balances of payments. At the present time the EEC's balance of payments is no more than the arithmetical sum of the balances of payments of its member-states: it is not a figure upon which the 'community' institutions are required to take policy decisions or action. The same is true of Comecon. But with unified monetary systems the group's balance of payments becomes a matter for community policy. To a large extent monetary unification settles the debate about common external policies decisively in favour of the Community approach. It can have an extremely powerful 'integrating' effect because policy decisions arising from balance of payments situations and therefore the international value of the integrated currencies must be taken in common. In a purely European context monetary unification is less likely to have immediate effects upon EEC policy than upon Comecon policy because the EEC's balance of payments with Comecon tends to be favourable and will probably remain so. However, with unitary monetary institutions the EEC will of necessity have to take common decisions about the volume and duration of credit granted to East Europe. Unless the tendency towards an adverse balance of payments situation on the Comecon side can be overcome by the diversification and expansion of exports a Comecon group policy under conditions of monetary unification may have to be restrictive and it is possible to imagine the member-states and the 'community' making a far greater use than they do today of tariffs as regulators of imports.

Monetary unification therefore occupies a uniquely critical position in that its adoption necessarily implies group strategies. There is no choice. Once it has occurred other aspects of external economic policy will inevitably become 'common' and the choice between pursuing common group strategies and allowing member-states to pursue strategies of their own will grow progressively narrower.

Monetary unification in Comecon if it is associated in, say, ten years' time with *full* convertibility of the rouble (i.e. a situation in which anyone can buy roubles, zloty or forints with foreign exchange and freely use the roubles, zloty or forints to buy Russian, Polish or Hungarian goods) must entail (*a*) a substantial increase in the operation of unplanned demand within the domestic economies of Eastern Europe and therefore further reforms in their planning systems and (*b*) the involvement of the rouble group of currencies in a multilateral world monetary system. The effect therefore will be to lift East–West relations in Europe to an ever-increasing extent from the European regional context into a world context.

This being so, we may expect the relations of the EEC with East European states or with Comecon as a whole to be conducted at three different levels. At the highest level, the EEC and Comecon participate in international discussion and negotiation of macro-economic conditions. In the second place, there are certain residual bilateral questions to be resolved by inter-Community negotiation; such things for example as the liberalisation of imports, trade agreements, credit policy, certain energy policies, agricultural policy, etc. But at the third level the role of Community institutions in the sphere of actual transactions, that is to say of actual buying and selling, is likely to be limited. The issue here is the role of the enterprise both in the EEC and in Comecon. If we are to see a growth of multilateralism in Europe it is vitally important that Eastern enterprises should be able to conduct transactions with Western enterprises. Otherwise if Western enterprises are always forced to do business in highly centralised ministries and other governmental institutions the temptation to rely to a greater and greater extent upon centralised intervention from the Western side will continually grow.

7 Political relations between East and West in Europe

The Europe within which the enlargement of the EEC is taking place has lived since 1945 in the aftermath of the Second World War, the ending of the West European overseas empires, the institutionalised Communist revolutions in Eastern Europe and the revolution of political sentiment in Western Europe which has made war between states in that part of the Continent unthinkable.

In historical perspective this post-war, post-imperial and post-revolutionary situation is still new. A quarter of a century or less is not time enough in which to recover from the shock of such profound changes or completely to discard attitudes of mind inherited from the remoter past or generated during the process of change itself. Most aspects of East–West relations in Europe are strongly influenced by 'defensive' attitudes on the part of all the actors: in the West defence of the democratic political system restored at the cost of millions of lives in war and by the immediate post-war reconstruction; in the East the defence of the post-war and post-revolutionary political, economic and social system. Cutting across these major lines of defence are others, such as the defence of national identity and interest, which may not always coincide with the main division of the continent.

The East–West division of Europe, although its frontiers are defined by differences in intellectual, political and social systems, is also territorial. The two social, economic and political systems inhabit compact geographical areas, and the defection of a state from one system to the other would appear as a territorial loss. However, while the division is, by accident of war, territorial, the acquisition of new territory by one system from the other by the use of force is not now a serious danger to peace. No government in Europe, East or West, has among its declared aims the forceful alteration of frontiers or the recovery of lost lands or peoples. Sharp though the differences are between East and West, it is probably true to say that neither side fears unprovoked armed aggression by the other in the interests of territorial aggrandisement within Europe itself.

Until 1969–1970 the USSR professed to see in West Germany a power dissatisfied with its frontiers, prepared sooner or later to take 'revanchist' action to regain what it had lost in war. The 'German problem' was at the heart of Europe's troubles. The initiatives taken by the West German government which led to the signing of the Soviet and Polish Treaties of 1970 and their ratification in May 1972 by the German Parliament constituted an important step towards a practical solution of that problem. The Soviet–German Treaty does not rule out the ultimate reunification of Germany but the formula adopted by Herr Brandt's government of one German nation and two German states relegates the question of reunification to a more distant future when the general European situation may be more favourable to reconsideration. The Treaty does not require Western Germany to give *de jure* recognition to East Germany. The agreement is to 'respect', not to 'recognise' frontiers, admittedly a somewhat equivocal formula but representing some shift in the position of the USSR, for, in exchanges with the Germans between 1966 and 1968, the Soviet government was insisting on the 'immutability' of frontiers and the recognition of the East German government. The Treaty renounces the use of force in the settlement of issues between the two countries, and the contracting parties pledge themselves to conduct their relations with each other in accordance with Article 2 of the UN Charter. No reference is made to Articles 53 and 107 (the enemy state clauses) in the Treaty, but in October, 1972 the four former occupying Powers—the USA, USSR, Britain and France—declared that they retained their rights and responsibilities for Germany as a whole. In a declaration of 29 July 1970, Mr. Gromyko said that the USSR as a victorious power has the right to intervene in Germany and yet has concluded a treaty under which disputes are to be settled *exclusively* by peaceful means. The treaty contains no reference to internal West German affairs. The West German government made the ratification of the Treaty conditional upon the conclusion of a new Four-Power agreement on Berlin. An agreement concluded by the USA, France, the USSR and the UK, the four powers concerned and welcomed by them all, was signed on 3 September 1971. It guarantees that transit traffic through Eastern Germany between West Berlin and the Federal Republic will be unimpeded that ties between West Berlin and the Federal Republic will be maintained and developed, and that communications between West Berlin and Eastern Germany will be improved. Ratification of the treaties by the German Parliament in May 1972 after a long struggle between Herr Brandt's government and the Christian Democrat opposition, allowed the signature of a general treaty on traffic between the two German states, and paved the way for signature of the protocol of the four-power agreement on Berlin.

In pursuit of the Berlin agreement the Soviet government moved with considerable speed, and seems to believe that it made substantial concessions in its negotiations with the West German government for the conclusion of the Soviet–German Treaty. Coupled with repeated calls for all-European co-operation, with a speech by Mr. Brezhnev in Paris in October 1971 decrying the policy of hostile blocs and his major policy speech in March 1972, suggesting a diminution in Soviet hostility to the Common Market, Soviet actions seem to imply an increasing willingness to accept realities and a growing trust in the good faith of the Western nations. The Treaties with Germany and the Berlin agreement were generally welcomed by the East European states. The Nato powers, including of course the United Kingdom, supported the West German government's initiatives and welcomed the signing and ratification of the Treaties with the USSR and Poland.

All these developments, although they still do not include a formal peace treaty with Germany, in effect provide a working alternative to such a treaty for the immediate future, a position largely negotiated by a Social Democrat German government working firmly within the framework of western alliances. From the Soviet side it does not appear that much pressure was put upon the German government to break its Western ties as the price of concluding a treaty. Whereas General de Gaulle's approaches to the East in the late sixties were made in the context of his quarrels with the USA, Nato, Britain and the EEC, Herr Brandt has carried the Western allies with him and engaged their interest in the new situation, a fact which ought to be reckoned an advantage by the USSR. On the other hand, the USSR has recognised the place of Western Germany within the Western system.

No reasonable person could suppose that even without the Treaties Western Germany would have attempted to secure reunification unilaterally and by force, or that a CDU government would make such an attempt. The renunciation of force in the Treaties is to that extent no more than a formal expression of an existing reality but if the USSR considers that the agreements confirm the reality and if in consequence the vitriolic language used in the past about Western Germany falls into disuetude and the 'German problem' is for the time being set aside, Europe gains time in which to move forward towards a more confident and rational future. There remains the question of Western 'recognition' of the East German State. On 8 November 1972, the two German States, after long drawn-out negotiations, initialled a general treaty which Herr Brandt, the West German Chancellor, affirmed would normalise relations between them and initiate an era of co-operation on the basis of equal rights. Its terms renounce the use of force, confirm the inviolability of the existing frontier, and pledge the two states to respect each other's territorial integrity and independence in internal and external affairs. The two States will exchange permanent representative missions. The treaty has still to be ratified but it would seem that its effect is that the two Germanies, without formally recognising each other as separate States, for most practical purposes accept each other's existence as independent entities. Assuming that the treaty is ratified and that a constructive dialogue between Western and Eastern Germany can be maintained, Western Germany will have done as much as lies within its power to dispose of real or imaginary Soviet and East European fears about its territorial ambitions to the East. The treaty between Western Germany and Poland, signed on 7 December 1970, affirmed that the Oder–Neisse boundary between the two countries established at the Potsdam Conference of August 1945 is the frontier and the two States renounced all territorial claims.

Within the western half of Europe there are four neutral states, Austria, Finland, Sweden and Switzerland, which, for reasons which differ between one state and another, are unwilling to commit themselves to West European alliances, but since their neutrality is real there is no likelihood whatever that they would adhere to the Eastern system. They do not constitute a 'territorial' problem. Territorially the postwar situation in Europe is, in effect, stable.

The political systems of the two halves of Europe must also be regarded as stable, in the sense that however much the political pendulum may swing in the nine states forming the EEC (and the same is true of the neutrals) it is highly improbable that any of them will adopt a Communist political system in the foreseeable future, or that however much the political system in Eastern Europe is modified by the gradual introduction of new legal norms or new forms of consensus politics and 'parliamentary' political activity, it will cease to be based upon a one-party system and the Leninist principle of 'democratic centralism'. The narrowness of the limits of Soviet tolerance for political change in Eastern Europe was decisively demonstrated in Czechoslovakia in 1968.

'Territorial' stability in Europe, so long as it persists unthreatened for a long period (say to the end of the century), may be presumed to be beneficial for European peace. The same cannot be said of the perpetuation of differences between the two major political systems although they must be accepted as a reality. Even if neither side is so filled with crusading zeal as actively to attempt large-scale political subversion of the other, if in other words both agree to 'co-exist', problems arising from the difference of the systems remain. In the long run the argument between Communist and non-Communist about the merits of democratic centralism or parliamentary democracy, about the place of man

78

in society, or about the necessity for a socialist transformation of free societies, will be settled by the actual performance of the two systems in providing for the welfare and in meeting the aspirations of their citizens. In the meantime we cannot reasonably hope for a dissolution of ideology differences, chiefly because ideology plays an important role in the defence of the existing social and political structures. Marx –Leninism at the present time may not be a serious competitor for majority political thought in Western Europe, although the situation could change if Western Europe were to plunge into severe economic recession, but in Eastern Europe it provides the philosophical justification for authoritarian government under a one-party system in the phase of transition to Communism. It is a 'revolutionary' doctrine which in theory interprets international relations in terms of class interest and the actions of other states and groups of states which do not belong to the socialist system in terms of an historical process which is destined to end in a socialist victory in the 'international class war'. So long as this kind of political thinking persists it is evident that the existence of 'international class enemies' can be used as the justification of the defence of the revolutionary achievement in the USSR and Eastern Europe not only by military and political means but also by intellectual discipline and authority. As successive party leaders in the USSR have said there can be no question of 'ideological co-existence'. The Soviet government and Party as the guardians of these doctrines in Europe are therefore almost inevitably conservative in their attitudes towards the newer Communist regimes in Eastern Europe and towards the non-Communist West, and will remain so for the foreseeable future. On the other hand the concepts of 'international class war' and the 'victory of socialism over capitalism', enshrined in innumerable contemporary Communist documents, and the legacy of revolutionary doctrine must continue to sustain uneasiness in the West about Soviet motives for a long time to come and maintain the defensiveness of Western attitudes to the USSR. It will require many more years of patient diplomacy and repeated demonstrations of good faith on both sides to dispel the underlying defensiveness of the two halves of Europe arising from the ideological differences.

The steps which have been taken in recent years to improve the political atmosphere in Europe have not weakened the boundaries between 'spheres of influence' within which Western and Eastern Europe live. It has yet to be shown that in signing its Treaty with Germany and in pressing so assiduously for a European Security Conference the USSR desires much more in Europe than stronger guarantees for the *status quo* in respect of its own sphere. This may prove to be an excessively cautious view. Time alone will prove or disprove it.

Soviet policy in regard to the cohesion of its European sphere of influence and the level of Soviet bloc military forces, although its effects may be seen most strikingly in Europe, is not of course solely determined by the situation in Europe. As a world power the USSR confronts the USA, China and to some extent Japan as well as the European members of Nato. Power relationships on the world scale are beginning to change. For most of the post-war period the critical relationship has been the 'bi-polar' balance between the USSR and the USA, Western Europe lying within the sphere of influence of the latter. Now, with the emergence of China as a nuclear power, the persistence of the Sino–Soviet dispute, the beginnings of rapprochement between the USA and China, uncertainties about the extent of the American military commitment to Europe and strains between the USA and Japan, the comparatively simple system of relationships between two super-powers appears to be dissolving into something far more complex. The high level of the Warsaw Pact countries' armaments, the rapid growth of Soviet maritime power, Soviet diplomatic advances in the Middle East and Southern Asia, have all to be looked at in the light of these new power relationships. The cohesion of the Soviet sphere of influence in Europe and the level of its defences is not by any means an exclusively European problem and questions of the balance of power and relations between spheres of influence in Europe cannot be resolved by Europeans acting alone. Nevertheless, especially as a result of deep-seated uncertainties about the extent of the long-term American commitment to Europe, the West European states are becoming increasingly impatient of the passive role which they have played in the world balance of power in the past quarter of a century, and there is a growing conviction that West Europe should establish some form of sphere of influence of its own in the evolving world situation. Exactly what this is to be is not yet clear. It is to be hoped that it will not entail a net addition to world armaments, a contingency which may be avoided by the economical and effective interlocking of the American and West European defence systems. Western Europe can in fact only be the gainer if the USA maintains its European commitments while at the same time steadily improving its relations with the USSR; it could only be the loser in a situation where the USA was seen to be withdrawing from its European commitments in a period of tension or uncertainty in its relations with the USSR.

In such circumstances, to expect power relationships in Europe in the immediate future to reflect only the political, economic and social relationships between the Western and Eastern states of Europe would be to take a myopic view. It is sometimes argued that Soviet policy towards Western Europe is determined by a desire to persuade Europeans to take precisely that view, so that at least this one continent may be quiescent in a turbulent world and the emergence of yet another major force be prevented by lulling Western Europe into neutrality or indifference to events outside. The Soviet government may not, perhaps, be blamed for entertaining such hopes even if in fact they are illusory, but this generation of West Europeans will be justly blamed by its descendants if it becomes 'Eurocentric' and refuses world responsibilities. It would for example be a retrograde step if Great Britain, after entering the Common Market, were to turn her back upon the Commonwealth. No doubt the political climate in Europe could be kept cool if the West European nations were to disregard the troubles of the world, particularly those of the developing countries, and concentrate their attention upon improving their own 'regional' prosperity and comfort. But a European influence in world affairs will not be restored by that method, for in the end it would destroy West Europe's nerve for action: its capacity for influence in Moscow and elsewhere would dwindle to nothing. In fact it seems almost inevitable that a Western Europe growing in economic strength, shedding its sense of guilt for past errors and growing in political confidence, will be driven to play a more active part in world politics. East–West relations in Europe, which in a purely regional framework might be conducted in a low key, will reflect to an increasing extent the state of power relations in the world as a whole and for that reason be subject to disturbance by the currents of events outside Europe.

Another potential cause of stress between the West European states and the USSR is the position of the non-Russian states in the Soviet sphere of influence. That this is not an issue likely to lead to war has been demonstrated repeatedly by the lack of Western economic or military response to events in Eastern Europe, especially Hungary in 1956 and Czechoslovakia in 1968, which aroused strong emotions in the West. It may well be that the virtual certainty of non-intervention by the West in such situations, should they again arise, is at least a guarantee against a European war. But to judge this issue solely in terms of armed conflict is to rely upon a crude and primitive criterion. Are we not, in looking for a 'new Europe', entitled to use more civilised judgments than that? Europe is hardly likely to be 'renewed' if the sole test of bad and good policies is whether they do or do not lead to war. If the affairs of a new Europe are to be managed pacifically by 'negotiation' and 'co-operation' and not by force, then conduct which destroys the confidence upon which such methods of management depend is unacceptable. The alternatives are clear: either all-European security must be negotiated on an all-European basis or if the security of one half of Europe is to be maintained by force there is almost nothing 'European' to negotiate about. Double standards are an impossible basis for the pacific management of the affairs of a continent. The total foreign policy of a state constitutes an indivisible whole. The credibility of the

USSR as a negotiating partner in Europe's affairs will be determined as much by what it does in Eastern Europe as by what it says in Western Europe.

The affairs of Eastern Europe are an integral part of any peaceful European scene. They are not something which the existence of a Soviet sphere of influence can exclude from the attention of West Europeans. Several Eastern and Western European states have common frontiers: distances are negligible in terms of modern communications: Berlin, Prague and Budapest are in fact nearer to Brussels than Rome; Warsaw only slightly more distant. Poorly though the history of the East European states is taught in Western Europe, enough is known for West Europeans to recognise their strongly marked national characteristics and cultures. The growth of tourism, even if it does little to foster understanding between the tourist and the toured, imprints the map of Eastern Europe ever more firmly upon the consciousness of the ordinary West European. Czechoslovakia may have appeared to Mr. Chamberlain, when he broadcasted to the British people in September 1938, a faraway country of whose people we knew nothing; it no longer appears so to any intelligent Briton in 1972. The maintenance of artificial barriers to communication between peoples in such close geographical contiguity in a small continent must therefore be one of the most vivid of indicators that all is not well with the peace of Europe. It is perhaps not too much to say that we may judge the health of Europe as a whole as much by the height and thickness of that barrier as by anything else. In a rational, secure, confident and co-operative Europe it should not exist at all, whatever the differences of ideology to the extent that it does exist the situation in Europe remains irrational, insecure, fear-ridden and unco-operative.

In the coming decades social change in Europe will exert increasing pressures upon the boundary between the two spheres of influence. As the standard of life, especially in Eastern Europe, rises and expectations rise faster still, the choice between alternative ways of getting and spending time and money will broaden. Eastern Europe is still only on the threshold of the age of 'consumer durables', especially of the family car and television set, which in Western Europe have so greatly enlarged the means and the appetite for real and vicarious travel. With the widespread use of these means of movement the political boundary between East and West which divides Europeans with common tastes and high levels of intelligence will appear more artificial and absurd to the ordinary man. The increasing scope for mobility is, as the Western European states already know, a social fact of major importance. Soon it will affect the whole of the continent and the pressure for the liberalisation of travel between East and West is likely in time to become irresistible.

The pressure for 'cultural' interchange, as a flow separate from other forms of contact, is unlikely to increase at the same rate as the pressure for freer movement if only because it interests much smaller sections of the population. It is at present largely controlled by governments through cultural agreements which seek to establish reciprocity in the exchange of scientists, scholars and artists passing between the states in the course of a year, either as short-term visitors or for longer periods of study and research. Universities and learned institutions in both Western and Eastern Europe add 'unofficial' exchanges to the official ones. In certain fields, such as many aspects of pure science, some aspects of technology, economics, management science, town planning and environmental studies, the interchange allows a continuing dialogue between Western and Eastern specialists, both sides conventionally avoiding political polemics, but it will fall very short of a free exchange of ideas between West and East until books, newspapers and radio programmes are as freely circulated between say the USSR and Western Europe as they are between the USA and Western Europe. This may be among the last of the European freedoms to be achieved.

Economic interchange between Western and Eastern Europe either in the form of conventional trade or industrial co-operation, as we have seen in earlier chapters, has been growing steadily if not spectacularly and may be expected to continue to grow in the same way. Moreover there has in recent years been a noticeable tendency for the discussion of economic problems in the two halves of the continent to find common ground and for methods of economic management to share common characteristics. Given that economic growth is a major priority for every European government, and that materialistic attitudes to life are widespread in both East and West, is it not possible that economics will provide an autonomous motive force beyond the powers of statesmen to arrest, which will shape a European political and social unity in all but name?

The interrelationships of economics and politics are so complex that it would be foolhardy to attempt a generalised answer to this question, but there are practical reasons why, although we may expect to obtain political and social gains from the development of economic relationships, we should not pitch expectations too high.

The rate of growth of economic interchange between even the most actively engaged of the West European states (France, Western Germany, Italy and the United Kingdom) and Eastern Europe has not been so great over the past two decades and is unlikely to be so great over the next two as to establish a condition of economic 'interdependence', that is to say a condition in which disengagement from trade and industrial co-operation would immediately damage economic welfare on both sides to an extent noticeable to the consumer. It would seem in fact that if the programme of Comecon is effective and a higher level of Comecon self-sufficiency is attained, economic 'interdependence' with Western Europe *in this sense* might actually decline, even though the level of exchanges with Western Europe were to rise in absolute terms.

Secondly, it is a matter of historical experience that levels of economic exchange and the state of political relations are not closely correlated. The Czechoslovak crisis made very little difference to the level of East—West trade; while the USSR was treating Western Germany as a 'revanchist' potential enemy the level of Soviet—German trade was rising. The Communist side has the authority of Lenin for the expansion of trade with the capitalist world regardless of ideological conflict. The philosophy of 'business is business' in all political weathers is only viable if those conducting business on each side accept the political and administrative conventions of the other and deliberately avoid any attempt to attach political strings to their transactions. At the intergovernmental level commercial policy cannot be effectively used as a political instrument. The idea that Western states should 'trade' commercial concessions on their side against the granting of political liberties on the Communist side is in fact impracticable; on the Western side deals have to be negotiated by private enterprises, to whom the combination of political and commercial activity are both unworkable and unacceptable; at the intergovernmental level it would soon become obvious to both sides that trade was being used politically and the result would be to heighten rather than diminish political conflict.

The concept of a convergence of the political and social systems of European states led by a convergence of their economic systems has certain intellectual attractions, but implies the withering away of one or both of the political philosophies that divide the Continent. It also underestimates the power of modern governments and the possibilities of economic 'success' under the two systems. If the capacity for economic growth and rising standards of life is the principal test of government, as it is at present, both the modified forms of central planning in Eastern Europe and the modified forms of market economy in Western Europe can claim success: on the basis of growth criteria alone there is no overwhelming pressure on either side to adopt the other's political and social system. Nor is there any strong *a priori* reason why a 'convergence' of economic systems between two or more states should radically alter their political relationships by an autonomous process requiring no conscious political act. Parallelism between the planned economies of Eastern Europe does not assure integration between them without an effort of political will; the creation of a customs union between similar types of economy in Western Europe demanded a major exercise of political will in the drawing up of the Treaty of Rome, and has left major political tasks still to be done. Convergence in the sense that there is increasing similarity between economic structures and the economic and social problems facing governments in both East and West Europe may indeed be occurring, but it has yet to be convincingly demonstrated that it has much relevance to inter-state politics. It is unlikely to determine the course of European politics in the lifetime of this generation of Europeans.

What may reasonably be expected from the growth of economic relations between Western and Eastern Europe is, firstly, the establishment of a wider area of mutual interest and confidence at governmental and sub-governmental levels and all that this implies in terms of habits and patterns of conduct; secondly, the extension of knowledge —since international business cannot be conducted in ignorance of the other man's rules, his political assumptions and his psychology; thirdly, to the extent that a common rationality is applied to economic problems in West and East, an enhancement of welfare and an improvement in the channels of intellectual communication; and lastly the possible establishment of new East–West institutions for handling particular economic problems, or the strengthening of existing ones, especially in banking and finance.

Advances of this sort towards common codes of conduct and improved communication between the peoples of Western and Eastern Europe in the economic sphere can be made without radical changes of political principles or institutions: in fact the advances are likely to be considerably slowed down unless people on both sides *accept* political diversity as the practical basis upon which economic negotiations and transactions take place. The growth of economic relations could actually help to prolong the difference of political outlook and institutions between Western and Eastern Europe rather than dissolve it. Trade and industrial co-operation do not offer practical short-cuts to political convergence if that is what is desired. But is it desired? Few West Europeans want their own political system to converge upon the Soviet system. It is equally clear that the USSR will do everything in its power to prevent the Communist political system from converging either upon existing political systems in Western Europe or upon any other system, socialist or not, short of the Marx–Leninist model.

Notwithstanding all the constraints upon the development of an 'open' all-European society which have been set out above, it is not totally unrealistic to hope for and to encourage more 'openness', defined as greater freedom to travel, to exchange the products of industry, and to communicate and discuss ideas, than exist today. What is ultimately needed is a common form of rationality which accepts that political, economic and social objectives may differ, that adherents of opposing views have the right to argue their case anywhere, that the merits of opposing ideologies will be proved or disproved by actual performance rather than by propaganda or censorship, that no continent can be said to be living in peace if it co-exists on either side of barbed wire fences, and finally that there is such a thing as 'Europe' in which all who live in the continent should enjoy certain rights as citizens.

Here the West European states have the initiative, since it is possible for them to construct their part of a European society in a liberal spirit and leave open an invitation to the East to join in the task of widening it. *General* relaxation of restrictions upon travel and the exchange of ideas could probably not be negotiated at a conference table, since under these conditions Western proposals for 'freedom' and 'openness', however well-meant, will appear to the East as politically offensive. Negotiation where it is applicable is more likely to be effective in particular cases, of which those concerning Berlin were an example. Western Europe is perhaps more likely to make the case for an open European Society in the limited sense used here by setting an example to the East, by contributing to the development of a common new rationality and demonstrating confidence in the justice and vitality of free political discussion, than by endeavouring to persuade the East to accept the idea as an item of a negotiated 'settlement'.

Europe has been a comparatively open continent more than once for particular classes of its citizens—for the soldier and administrator of the Roman Empire, for the scholars, Churchmen and chivalry of the Middle Ages, for the aristocracies of the eighteenth and early nineteenth centuries. To some extent it is becoming more open now for the scientist and technologist but the principal social pressures in this age are likely to come from the comparatively affluent 'common man' impatient of constraints upon his freedom to see and judge for himself. If there is to be a wider Europe it will be for him.

The concept of a single Europe in which people are free to travel, to do business and exchange ideas regardless of the political regime under which they live is obviously beset with difficulties, but any regime which is afraid to expose itself to currents of critical thought, to comparison, to contacts with other ways of life, is deliberately cutting itself off from the community of European peoples. It may be geographically part of Europe: it may take a formal part in the diplomatic affairs of the continent: but it does not belong to a European society in any real sense.

In the past decade and a half communication between the peoples of Western and Eastern Europe has somewhat improved but the concept of a single Europe has gained little ground. The Soviet conception of a settled and co-operative European continent appears to be based much more upon 'pan-European' than 'one-European' arrangements. A pan-

European system means the *addition* of new international treaties, agreements and institutions to the existing arrangements between states without breaking down the controls exercised by governments over economic development, trade exchanges, travel and intellectual communication. The USSR views with suspicion the concept of a more 'open' Europe which has been touched upon in this chapter and which, to judge by the pronouncements of West European political leaders and the North Atlantic Council, is favoured in principle by the Western states. Greater 'openness' as advocated by the West, and which in the long run if the argument of this chapter is accepted, will be the sign of political health in Europe, is at the present time interpreted by the USSR as licence for 'imperialist' subversion of the Eastern political system. And of course there is no gainsaying that freedom to travel, to transact business and to communicate ideas would expose the political systems of both East and West in Europe to severe tests. The concept of some kind of 'one-European society' is full of risks to both sides. For many years to come, advocacy of an 'open', one-Europe approach to the problems of the Continent will be set against advocacy of a pan-European approach. It may be proved in practice that the two are not mutually exclusive even if in principle there is still a wide gap between them. For example, a pan-European Committee concerning itself with environmental problems, although composed of representatives of states with different social systems, might, in order to be effective, have to work upon a one-Europe basis within its own field, thereby creating a small 'European society' of specialists unencumbered by ideological differences, or political controls, obeying a common rationality in pursuit of a common objective. The proliferation of such specialist 'societies', though formally pan-European, could, whether the effect was intended or not, gradually extend the openness between the two halves of the continent to which the one-European approach is directed, Gradualness and pragmatism may be the best way of escape from ideological postures.

For the most part this chapter has been concerned with very long-term issues. The truth is that almost every issue in Europe, within the Western half, within the Eastern half and between the two *is* long-term. Dramatic as the normalisation of West Germany's relation with Eastern Europe, or the summoning of a European security conference may seem to be, they can be no more than steps towards the solution of fundamental social, economic and political issues which keep Europe divided in the sense that its peoples do not live as neighbours in a European society. The effect of creating a 'new' Western Europe upon European East–West relations has to be considered in this light.

8 The enlarged EEC and East–West political relations in Europe

The possible impact of the enlargement of the EEC upon future political relations between Western and Eastern Europe may be considered in terms of: (a) the very short period covering the preparation for and holding of a European Security Conference in 1973; (b) the short period—the duration of which cannot be defined until the Conference has actually taken place—in which the consequences of the Conference are being assessed and any follow-up action put in train; and (c) a much longer period, in which fundamental issues between the Western and Eastern systems are, or are not, resolved.

It will be surprising if the enlarged EEC can make a dramatic impact upon East–West relations in the very short period. It will have been formally enlarged in January 1973, perhaps only a short time before the Conference opens, and although a 'summit' meeting of the nine members of the enlarged Community was held in October 1972, the political structure of the new Community is still a matter of debate, not to say controversy. It seems highly improbable within so short a period, especially as the USA will be involved in the Conference, and did not a little to bring the project to fruition by its joint statement with the USSR at the end of the Moscow summit conference in May, that any major change in European–American relations within the North Atlantic Council, or in the co-ordination of West European and American viewpoints, will occur before the Conference opens. The uncommitted West European nations will also be represented at the Conference with points of view of their own which neither the enlarged EEC nor the Atlantic partnership will wish to ignore. When this book was being written, the agenda of the Conference had not been drawn up so that it is out of the question to speculate upon its proceedings or to hazard a guess as to its outcome.

This being said however, the mere fact that the enlargement of the

EEC will have taken place before the Conference assembles must have a significance for the discussion of long-term issues which, no matter how the Conference is conducted, will lie at the root of all that is said and done in Helsinki. It immediately presents the USSR with the problem of indicating, if only in the most general way, its future attitudes towards West European integration and therefore its attitude to the future structure of Europe.

The enlargement of the EEC having already taken place, there will obviously be no point in Soviet tactics before, at, or after the Conference designed to prevent its enlargement. That issue, which has given rise to very bitter language from Moscow over the past decade, will be settled; one source of East–West disputation will be dried up. It does not necessarily follow that the USSR will cease to try to dissuade the neutrals and other West European states from closer association with the enlarged Community but there is nothing more it can do to prevent the new Community itself from growing in size. Since the general improvement of East–West relations in Europe must proceed at least in part by the gradual elimination of causes of contention, the removal of this one by the action of West European states themselves is a net gain. It is evident from Mr. Brezhnev's speech of 20 March 1972 that the USSR recognises an irreducible core of unity in Western Europe, and may be preparing to adjust its policies accordingly.

Mr. Brezhnev's remarks did not, however, suggest that acceptance of the new reality automatically implies juridical recognition of the enlarged EEC by the USSR; he coupled Eastern acceptance of the EEC with an unspecified acknowledgement by the EEC of the existing situation in Eastern Europe, and in so doing put the West on notice that Soviet recognition of the EEC may be presented as part of a bargain of some kind; but, before the Conference takes place, it is already evident that the concept of pan-European co-operation as an *alternative* to West European integration is dead. If such co-operation is to be further developed it has to start from the premise that an enlarged Community will participate in it. In its enlarged form, and given some practical and effective method of reaching common foreign policies where they are necessary, the EEC should be able to enter the new phase of East–West discussions confident that a West European community has been 'made' and cannot be unmade. A weakness of political 'blocs', which may cause them to act aggressively or unco-operatively in external relations, is fear of internal disintegration. Enhanced confidence in the cohesiveness of the group will give the enlarged EEC greater scope for manoeuvre, for experiment and for liberal policies.

In the very short period the primary issue may very well be whether the Conference itself is to be a once-for-all meeting or the matrix of new and continuing forms of East–West dialogue. For the Western side at least, a Conference cannot possibly be counted a success, or may even be counted a dangerous failure, if the Soviet intention is merely to engage in an exchange of generalities and retire with a string of signatures to a document or series of documents permanently enshrining social, political, economic and military spheres of influence in their present form. The communique issued at the end of the talks between President Nixon and the Soviet leaders in May 1972 (summarised in Appendix II) illustrates the level of generality on broad political issues which characterises such exchanges. It remains to be seen whether a Conference can give a sharper definition to the European issues which may constitute the basis of follow-up action.

There is no certainty that the USSR will choose to concentrate upon generalisation or that it is entirely free to do so if such an approach were to imperil the outcome of the Conference. Total failure of a Conference, in the sense that it ended abruptly with a restatement of fixed positions and the return home of delegations with nothing better to show than frustration and annoyance, would cause intense disappointment among the non-Russian states of Eastern Europe which have for many years unanimously supported the calling of the Conference and have in their own national foreign policies done as much as they could to persuade the Western states to accept it. Indeed, from December 1964, when Poland proposed to the General Assembly of the United Nations that a European conference should be convened until Mr. Gromyko affirmed Soviet support in Rome in April 1966, almost all the running was made by the smaller East European states without much outward sign of Soviet enthusiasm. Because at different times the East European states have put forward a variety of reasons for holding the conference, many of them contradictory, it is not easy to identify a single common purpose behind their sponsorship, but it would appear that all of them hope that in an atmosphere of *détente* and associated with pan-European proceedings as sovereign national states sitting at the same table as members of the EEC, non-committed and neutral Europeans, the Americans and Canadians, they will demonstrate their enduring right, written over and over again into such formal documents as the Warsaw Pact, the statutes of Comecon and its 1971 programme, to maintain an independent presence on the European scene and retain bilateral contact with the states of the non-Communist world. Both the USSR and the Western states know that this is the position; it is unlikely that the Soviet government would wish to take unilateral action either during the run-up to a conference, during a conference, or in its aftermath, which could saddle it with responsibility for the failure of an initiative which its allies have so ardently desired. To avoid this the USSR must respect Eastern European opinions, for it can hardly want to find itself surrounded in future by resentful allies in Eastern Europe and increased 'security' problems in its own sphere of influence.

The USSR, although appearing inflexible to Western eyes in its manner of dealing with the Eastern European states, has in fact changed its attitude to them more than once since 1956, the two factors determining its conduct being on the one hand its appreciation of the state of the Western alliance, and on the other hand its appreciation of the 'security' position in Eastern Europe. Between 1966 and 1968 the situation appeared reassuring in both respects—in the West Nato was in crisis and political advance in Western Europe at a standstill; in the East reforming zeal was being devoted to the economic rather than the political system and the ever-present fear of chaos was somewhat relaxed. In this period the affairs of Eastern Europe could be handled with a light rein. The Czechoslovak crisis of 1968 which above all suggested to Moscow that the one-Party system in that country was breaking down, reawakened the slumbering fears of political chaos and caused the rein to be tightened, in the sense that Soviet action in Czechoslovakia served as a clear warning to other East European states of the limits of Soviet tolerance. But to make this political lesson more palatable the USSR has permitted multilateral procedures in Eastern Europe to grow in number and significance. The method of drawing up the comprehensive programme of Comecon and recent proceedings of the Political Committee of the Warsaw Treaty Organisation bear the marks of the non-Russian states. Moreover, although the present attitude of the USSR seems to favour greater centralisation and uniformity in the area, Moscow endeavours to exercise restraints upon national divergencies—so long as they do not threaten the basic political structure—as unobtrusively as possible. The 'new' situation facing the USSR, and one which it cannot control, is the strengthening of the West European position by the enlargement of the EEC.

For its part the EEC will come to a conference table with the task of establishing a political community scarcely begun; it can hardly have resolved by the spring or early summer of 1973 the question of the relationship between Community external policies and the bilateral external policies of its member states. To present a united front during the proceedings it will need to reach a consensus of specifically community views of at least a minimal kind in advance. It will also need to decide what role Community institutions, in particular the Commission, will play at the Conference table. Unless the Security Conference is to consist in an exchange of platitudes it must give sharper definition to the Soviet and East European 'pan-European' approach to the future shape of Europe on the one hand, and the rather imprecise 'one Europe' approach of the Western states on the other. For a Western position on these lines to be formulated and defended at a major conference it will need to be carefully co-ordinated and sustained on a common basis throughout. It would clearly be bad for the new Community of Nine and for the conference itself if serious cracks between the positions of the EEC states were to become apparent. The Conference should in principle serve as a caralyst for a common EEC position and give additional momentum to the creation of consensus methods of policy formation in the new Community. The East European states on their side will obviously need to maintain consultation and joint action for the same reasons.

In the very short period, therefore, the interplay between the constituent states on both sides will have an important part in shaping the exchanges between the two sides. The Security Conference itself is not likely to be a confrontation between a Western side unanimous on all issues and an Eastern side unanimous on all issues. For this reason alone minimum rather than maximum common Western and common Eastern positions are likely to emerge.

Assuming that a Conference decides to establish procedures and institutions for more thorough investigation and negotiation of particular aspects of intra-European relationships and establish specialised East–West committees for that purpose, the longer-term issues of principle will begin to be dominant. On the EEC side one of the major issues will be its own general international role. In the East–West context the question will arise whether the European dialogue is to be conducted by new and specifically European institutions on both sides, or whether it will in essentials remain the business of the North Atlantic Council in the West and the Political Committee of the Warsaw Treaty Organisation in the East, both of which involve the superpowers. However the West European states arrange to conduct their own affairs, they are faced with the certainty that the East European combination will include the USSR.

The British White Paper on 'The United Kingdom and the European Communities', published on 7 July 1971, makes no direct reference to East–West relations in Europe although it quotes with approval a statement by Mr. Wilson in May 1967 when he was Prime Minister: 'a Europe that fails to put forward its full economic strength will never have the political influence which I believe it could and should exert within the United Nations, within the Western Alliance, and as the means for effecting a lasting *détente* between East and West. . .' These, says the White Paper, are common objectives of the Six, best pursued by common endeavour. One half of the political case for 'joining Europe' is that it will enable the UK and the Community to work for common objectives: the other is that 'it will make us and our European neighbours stronger to defend our national interests'. 'It is inevitable', says the White Paper at another point, 'that the scope of the Community's policies should broaden as member countries' interests become harmonised'. The UK joins at a moment when it will be able to influence the development of the co-ordination of foreign policy.

It will be a matter of judgment in the short period whether a particular type of negotiation with Eastern Europe should be conducted on a Community basis, on a Nato basis or by a member-state acting alone. The most important single East–West issue has hitherto been relations between the USSR and Federal Germany, which in the past two years has been handled bilaterally between the two countries (although with Nato approval), and it is difficult to see how Chancellor Brandt's Ostpolitik could have been presented or negotiated on a 'community' basis on behalf of the Federal Republic. The negotiating group could hardly have excluded the USA and the UK and would therefore in any case have been based upon Nato rather than the EEC. Moreover, the Federal Republic made the signature of its pact with the USSR conditional upon an agreement on Berlin, a four-power question involving neither Nato nor the Community directly.

If from a successful outcome of the Soviet–German dialogue political benefits can now be generalised to both halves of the continent, the need to use a bilateral approach to a problem of this magnitude may not arise again—except that the main responsibility for establishing new relationships between Western and Eastern Germany will rest primarily upon the governments of the two states, however deeply the other states of Western and Eastern Europe are concerned in the issue.

The British view of the short term requirements of foreign policy co-ordination as expressed in the White Paper is that 'the practical obligations which the UK will assume if we join now will involve no more than we have already assumed in WEU' (West European Union). Where on the scale between the bilateral operations of single states, the multilateral operations of West European institutions (WEU and Ministerial meetings) and the multilateral operations of the Council of Nato, any particular issue of foreign policy will be initiated and policy decisions taken, remains to be seen; but the distribution of responsibility between the three levels could be made according to the nature of the case and the strength of the interests involved, with the West European tier gradually strengthening its influence in an Atlantic framework.

The assumption underlying this forecast is that the USA remains involved in European affairs. The reassurances given by President Nixon to his Nato allies, especially to Chancellor Brandt during his visit to Washington in December 1971, and the references to Europe in the communique issued by the USA and USSR at the conclusion of the Summit talks in May indicate that the Nixon government intends to remain engaged in Europe. So long as this remains true and defence responsibilities are shared between Europe and the USA, major issues of policy towards Eastern Europe—even if a common West European viewpoint is established between the EEC member-states—will continue to be considered in a Nato context, or more informally, in discussions between Western Europe and the USA. The existence of an 'Atlantic' reference point beyond the European 'summit' and the likelihood that for many years to come the EEC states will also be engaged in bilateral exchanges with the USA may retard the establishment of common EEC foreign policy institutions. The maintenance of bilateral dialogues between EEC member-states and other countries outside Nato (for example, Australia, Japan or India) will have a similar effect. For the EEC states to abandon political bilateralism with the USSR and Eastern Europe altogether requires that they should abandon it in relation to the USA, Canada, Australia, Japan, India, Israel and other states outside the 'socialist commonwealth' which have their own bilateral relations with the USSR. Complete unification of foreign policy means unification in relation to *all* third countries. Nothing that has occurred in past discussion of political unification in Western Europe or that has been said by the British or EEC states during the debates on British entry suggests that such a development is imminent.

What is to be hoped for in the short term is that the enlarged EEC will develop a serviceable and intimate system of consultation and co-ordination of foreign policy operating either independently or, wherever appropriate, within the North Atlantic Alliance (notably in the matter of armaments) and the major international institutions both political and economic (UN, GATT, IMF) and that it will create such foreign policy institutions of its own as will permit consultation and co-ordination to operate effectively. To judge from recent pronouncements by French and British political leaders there is a strong school within the Nine thinking on these lines.

Relations with Eastern Europe in a purely European context will be only one, and not necessarily the most important, of the influences shaping an EEC foreign policy and its related institutions. The EEC of the Six gave a more convincing demonstration of unity in reaction to the American devaluation and imposition of import charges in 1971 than any it has ever given in relation to Eastern Europe. The beginnings of an EEC Mediterranean policy has been apparent in recent years—expressed in terms of commercial agreements but implying a belief that the Mediterranean area has a special political significance for Western Europe. Agreements giving Tunisia and Morocco a form of association with the EEC were concluded in 1969, Greece and Turkey having obtained theirs in 1961 and 1963 respectively (although the Greek association is to a large extent ineffective because of the political situation in that country). Malta concluded an association agreement in 1970, Israel and Spain have limited preferential trade agreements. The UAR, Lebanon and Cyprus have negotiations with the EEC in train, while Yugoslavia concluded a trade agreement in 1970. Although such agreements fall very far short of an EEC political presence in the Mediterranean, they represent, taken together, an expression of special EEC interest in an area where American and Soviet strength is already deployed. The USA has already voiced criticisms of a preferential area in the Mediterranean Recently EEC states have shown signs of speaking with one voice on Middle Eastern affairs in the United Nations.

It has yet to be seen how the accession of Britain to the EEC will affect her economic and political relationships with the countries of the Commonwealth and their relations with the enlarged Community. Commonwealth preferences will not expire until January 1975 and in the interval the African members will have the opportunity to decide whether, or how, they wish to associate with the new Community. The question of relations with Asian members of the Commonwealth and the 'old' Commonwealth has yet to be resolved. Much will depend upon the manner in which Britain in her new setting interprets her responsibility towards them, but if the links remain Britain may find herself engaged in a new chain of relationships between the Community and the overseas British connexions.

This is not the place in which to enlarge upon the potential world role of a new EEC; the relevance of the foregoing comments to the subject of the present study is that: (a) the formation of EEC foreign policy procedures and institutions will be determined in part by the impact of issues lying outside the European framework; (b) in consequence the procedures, institutions and modes of policy-formation brought into play by the EEC in future discussions with Eastern Europe will have an intrinsic life of their own and owe only part of their character to the European East–West dialogue itself; (c) the East –West European dialogue is likely to an increasing extent to take place in a world framework involving the interests of countries associated in one way or another with the member states and therefore with the Community also.

Although community of interest in extra-European affairs among the EEC states is still at an early stage, knowledge of its existence should serve to strengthen the cohesion of the enlarged EEC as it comes to grips with the short-term problems of relations with Eastern Europe. And in the short-term, as it threads its way through the East–West labyrinth, the enlarged EEC may often have to remind itself of community of interest in other fields, external and internal. For although negotiation with the USSR and Eastern Europe should in principle act as a catalyst for the co-ordination of EEC policies, the USSR is likely in the management of its own part in East–West negotiation to avoid conduct which would actually provoke a 'defensive' closing of EEC ranks. The USSR will on any count have most to gain from adopting a reasonable and pacific tone in discussion with the West—pressing for co-operation within the framework of existing frontiers and social systems, critical of 'discrimination', opposing intervention in the internal affairs of any state (with Eastern Europe particularly in mind), offering perhaps the establishment of pan-European institutions, but leaving the initiative for any fundamental change to come from the West. Now it is inherently more difficult for a group to decide upon the nature, content and presentation of an initiative, and to sustain it coherently in the face of rebuffs, than it is to defend an established position. To cause difficulty on the Western side over any Western proposal which it dislikes, the USSR has no need to display, or require its allies to display, crass and intolerable hostility; all it needs to do (something well within its power) is to withdraw into its shell and leave the West with the problem of dealing with a vacuum. The cohesion of an EEC policy towards Eastern Europe could be severely tested by this means.

The failure of a European Security Conference, in the sense that it ended without any provision for a continuing examination of Western or Eastern initiatives or any sign of willingness to consider fundamental change in the social relationships of the peoples of the Continent, could cause lasting damage; and it is for this reason that many responsible people in the West have questioned the wisdom of holding it. Whether it will do more good than harm has yet to be proved. But, being committed, the Western side will presumably be in agreement at least upon the necessity of securing follow-up action. To judge from Nato pronouncements, the Western side (or at least the Atlantic powers) hope, in the follow-up period, to secure greater freedom of exchanges between the peoples of Western and Eastern Europe and also to create a climate of confidence in which total military force levels may be reduced. The nature of Soviet proposals is as yet unknown. Clearly the Western side will need to be on its guard against any attempt to drive a wedge between the USA and the EEC, to lure West Europe into a false sense of security, or to obscure the discussion of fundamental issues.

In the short, as in the very short, period, it is not to be expected that the enlargement of the EEC will work miracles, but in the course of say five or six years it is to be expected that the particular contribution of the new grouping to the resolution of long-term problems should begin to be apparent.

The first of these issues is the relationship between the nation state and the integrating group in both East and West. All states in Western

Europe, including the EEC, believe that the East European states should retain their identity: all states in Eastern Europe hope to see the West European states retain theirs. The motives which lead to tacit agreement on this issue may differ considerably, but agreement exists. Yet appeals from either side to national sentiment on the other is interpreted either, as was General de Gaulle's appeal to Polish nationalism in 1967, as a Western attempt to disrupt the 'Socialist Commonwealth' or, as are Soviet appeals to the sentiment of smaller West European states, as a device to prevent the consolidation of Western Europe. There is a dilemma for both sides.

It is reasonable to assume that the more closely co-ordinated the EEC states become the more likely it is that the Eastern states will respond by presenting a common front, inevitably dominated by the USSR, but the member-states of the EEC are unlikely to allow their internal policies and objectives to be determined to any major degree by consideration of their possible effects upon the organisation and policies of Eastern Europe. No state or group of states, faced with internal problems such as those which face the EEC, could surrender a significant part of the initiative to other powers in this way. Nor is it likely that the states of Eastern Europe will allow their own discussion of internal relationships to be influenced in a major degree by the possible repercussions of their decisions upon the organisation of the EEC. On both sides individuals, groups and possibly entire states may from time to time remind fellow-members of the two groups of this problem, but the solution of internal questions is always likely to have priority.

In the sphere of East–West relations in Europe the distinction between 'inward-looking' and 'outward-looking' attitudes and policies on the EEC's part can be misleading. To ask the EEC to be so 'outward-looking' as to surrender control of the development of its internal structures to the force of external opinion is to be unreasonable. To expect 'outward-looking' policies, even if carried to the length of such a surrender, to bring immense and durable rewards from Eastern Europe, is to over-estimate the value of the rewards Eastern Europe could give. The principal 'reward' to be obtained from any policy in this sphere at the present time is a stable peace, of which good social relationships between the peoples of Western and Eastern Europe are an integral and vital part. The establishment of such a peace must be worked out between two halves of the continent which for technical reasons are becoming more closely integrated; the prospects for peace would indeed be poor if they were dependent upon halting or reversing this process. On the other hand, to push economic and political integration in either half of the continent beyond what is internally necessary solely in order to demonstrate strength, cohesion and defensive capacity to the other, would be to put the establishment of a stable peace at risk. Excessive preoccupation with East–West relations in Europe, if it were to lead to this kind of thinking, would be worse than treating them in a low key.

The desire for 'spontaneous' political unification in the EEC, that is to say, the creation of powerful political institutions as a matter of principle rather than for the achievement of immediately recognisable and specific aims, is weak in Western Europe at the present time. The 'political revolution' in Western Europe since 1945, which has convinced most West Europeans that war between West European states is unthinkable, is itself partly responsible for the general indifference to political unification, since it may seem that if West European states can live peaceably together without an elaborate political super-structure such a super-structure has no useful purpose to serve. A large part of the argument needed to persuade the British House of Commons to vote for entry into the EEC and to mitigate the suspicions of the British electorate, rested upon the evidence that the existing members of the EEC have palpably not lost their national sovereignty. As the White Paper put it: 'The Community is no federation of provinces or counties. It constitutes a Community of great and established nations, each with its own personality and traditions. The practical working of the Community accordingly reflects the reality that sovereign governments are represented round the table. . . There is no question of any erosion of essential national sovereignty; what is proposed is a sharing and an enlargement of individual national sovereignties in the general interest.'

It is the nature of the 'general interest' which is crucial to this approach. It implies that by sharing resources and pooling authority in joint enterprises of varying magnitude, the use of a Community method will demonstrably add more to the welfare of the citizens of the community than could be added by the independent enterprise of separate states using their own resources and national authority. However the principle is applied, whether wholesale or step by step, each addition to the scope of Community enterprise requires adjustment in the exercise of sovereignty by the member-states. The process therefore continually raises the question of the purpose and value of the nation state in late twentieth century Europe.

There are those throughout Western Europe who, disillusioned by horrors perpetrated not so long since in the name of nationalism in Western Europe itself and outraged by the sheer silliness to which the expression of national differences so frequently descend, consider the nation state to be an evil. Few West Europeans today could find anything to commend in the irrational hatreds, prejudices and ambitions of national states which have led to European wars. But there is another side to the coin, more clearly perceived perhaps in Eastern than in

Western Europe at the present time. It is that in a world growing technologically more uniform and vulnerable to bureaucratic dictatorship, variety of life-styles is a defence of liberty. The variety of national life-styles has made immense contributions to the art, literature, architecture, philosophy, music and landscape which are a major part of the European heritage. It is no accident that uniformity and regimentation are characteristic of societies under dictatorship. If variety of national life-style can form a defence against the grey uniformity upon which authoritarianism depends, it is not lightly to be thrown away. How the enlarged Community will reconcile the demands of national life-styles with those of the large-scale technological society will be watched with interest and concern in Eastern Europe, for the pattern established by the EEC will influence the solution of comparable problems in that part of the Continent far more deeply than exhortation. There would be a valid case for 'inward-looking' upon this issue on the part of the EEC if the result of introspection were to be the establishment of a pattern acceptable on its own merits to the more liberal spirits in Eastern Europe. What the EEC does to resolve its own internal problems may have greater effects upon the situation in Eastern Europe and relations between Eastern and Western Europe in the long run than the construction of a self-conscious Community 'Ostpolitik'.

It goes without saying, in the second place, that if the enlarged Community is to encourage the growth of multilateral contacts between Eastern and Western Europe it must demonstrate convincingly that multilateralism and openness in the economic, social and political spheres are successful, in terms of welfare and personal liberty, within its own frontiers.

The EEC will, whether deliberately or not, provide a long-term demonstration for Eastern Europe in the economic field—not merely in terms of growth for in this respect the East European states are probably satisfied that they can do as well as anyone—but if the enlarged EEC can show that private initiative acting effectively upon rational microeconomic criteria within a broadly market system can sustain growth, reward enterprise and labour justly, and provide stability in the level of prosperity without ever-increasing intervention by state or community institutions, it will strengthen the case for liberal economic experiment in Eastern Europe. If it fails it may easily strengthen the case for economic authoritarianism. The manner in which it conducts its external affairs is closely related to the conduct of its internal affairs. By exercising the greatest possible flexibility in handling economic transactions, by giving the greatest possible scope for negotiations and transactions below the level of the national and community institutions, by eschewing the adoption of centralisation for doctrinaire reasons and by avoiding the device of using 'strong' external policies to remedy internal weakness, the enlarged EEC may encourage a similar flexibility and variety on the East European side.

Thirdly, for the pattern of EEC economic, social and political life to have any influence upon the future shape of East–West relations, the enlarged EEC must be coherent and strong. Without coherence and strength it cannot pursue liberal policies. An individual or a state which surrenders the initiative and grants concessions because no other course is possible is not liberal but weak. To act liberally clearly implies that the actor has consciously chosen a liberal course although he has the capacity to do otherwise. In the comparatively primitive times in which we live it is also necessary to command power in order to be listened to. Lastly, a weak and divided political organisation provides a perpetual invitation to the ill-disposed to meddle in its affairs and thereby generate international insecurity. The Community must command respect both from its own citizens and from its neighbours; to do this it must both perform well and be seen to possess a reserve of power even if power is not continually displayed. Having set out upon the course of establishing a Community in Western Europe, the states of EEC cannot allow the enterprise to fail, for failure would expose the whole European situation, and not least the East–West situation, to a renewal of manoeuvres and intrigue designed to involve the 'disintegrated' EEC states in new power-combinations and put the structure of Europe into a melting-pot from which no one knows what substance might flow.

The resolution of these internal problems and the establishment of an 'attractive' political economic and social model for Europe is probably the best unique contribution which an enlarged EEC can make in the long run to the improvement of East–West relations in Europe. A Community which is prosperous, democratic, liberal, flexible and confident and, while enlarging the sphere of the general interest, also values and respects the variety of national and regional life-styles within its borders, and is prepared for rational dialogue with other states or groups of states and for the free exchange of ideas, goods, services and people, in the knowledge that its own performance is good enough to stand up to criticism and comparison, would indeed be something 'new' in Europe and present a pattern of conduct which no European state East or West could ignore.

Table Appendix I   THE GROWTH OF TRADE BETWEEN COMECON AND WESTERN EUROPE 1955–1971*

Year	Total W Europe/Comecon		Total EEC/Comecon†		Total EFTA/Comecon‡		Share of total West Europe/Comecon	
	Value ($m)	Increase (%)	Value ($m)	Increase (%)	Value ($m)	Increase (%)	EEC/Comecon (%)	EFTA/Comecon (%)
1955–1957§	2 922	—	1 043	—	1 063	—	35·7	36·4
1958	3 372	15·4	1 325	26·9	—	—	39·9	·—
1959	3 771	18·8	1 530	9·6	—	—	40·6	—
1960	4 527	20·1	1 920	25·5	1 300	—	42·6	28·7
1961	4 824	6·5	2 140	11·5	1 470	13·1	44·3	30·5
1962	5 239	8·5	2 305	7·7	1 790	21·8	44·0	34·2
1963	5 635	7·6	2 320	0·7	1 900	6·1	41·2	33·7
1964	6 050	7·3	2 510	8·2	2 020	6·3	41·5	33·4
1965	7 010	15·9	2 850	13·5	2 240	10·9	40·7	31·9
1966	8 050	14·8	3 430	20·4	2 530	12·9	42·6	31·8
1967	8 920	10·8	4 050	18·1	2 690	6·3	41·3	30·2
1968	9 550	8·2	4 440	9·6	2 920	8·6	46·4	30·6
1969	10 610	9·9	5 110	13·1	3 940	26·1	48·2	38·1
1970	11 300	6·1	5 810	12·2	4 440	11·3	51·4	39·3
1971	13 800	19·6	7 040	17·5	4 720	6·4	51·0	34·2

Source: United Nations, *Monthly Bulletin of Statistics*, Special Table C.

* Trade totals shown are arrived at by adding together the value of exports from the West European and the Comecon sides.
† Excluding trade between Western and Eastern Germany.
‡ Excluding Finland.
§ Average.

Appendix II

'Basic Principles of relations between
the United States of America and the
Union of Soviet Socialist Republics'

These were set out in the joint communiqué issued at the end of the summit talks between President Nixon and the Soviet leaders in Moscow on 29 May 1972. The full text was published in the British press on 30 May 1972: the following is a summary of some of the main points contained in the 12 heads of agreements.

1. In the nuclear age there is no alternative to conducting Societ–American relations on the basis of peaceful co-existence. Differences in ideology and social systems are not obstacles to the bilateral development of normal relations.

2. The USA and the USSR will do their utmost to avoid military confrontations and to prevent the outbreak of nuclear war. The prerequisites for maintaining peaceful relations between the two countries are the recognition of their security interests based on the principle of equality and the renunciation of the use or threat of force.

3. The two countries will seek to promote conditions in which all countries will live in peace and will not be subject to outside interference in their internal affairs.

4. The USA and USSR will widen the juridical basis of their mutual relations and ensure that bilateral agreements concluded between them and multilateral treaties and agreements to which they are jointly parties are faithfully implemented.

5. The USA and USSR are ready to continue the practice of exchanging views at the highest level and will facilitate

contacts between representatives of the legislative bodies of the two countries.

6. The two countries will continue their efforts to limit armaments on a bilateral and multilateral basis. Their ultimate objective is the achievement of complete disarmament and the establishment of an effective international security system in accordance with the principles of the United Nations.

7. The USA and USSR will promote the growth of bilateral commercial and economic relations between the two countries.

8. Mutual contacts in the fields of science and technology will be developed.

9. The two sides reaffirm their intention to deepen cultural ties with one another.

10. To give a permanent character to these ties the USA and the USSR will establish joint commissions or other joint bodies wherever feasible.

11. The USA and the USSR recognise the sovereign equality of all states.

12. These basic principles do not affect any obligation with respect to other countries earlier assumed by the USA and USSR.

The following references to European issues were contained in the joint communiqué issued on 29 May 1972 at the conclusion of the summit talks:

1. Both sides took note of favourable developments in the relaxation of tensions in Europe.

2. They intend to make further efforts to ensure a peaceful future for Europe.

3. They agree that the territorial integrity of all states in Europe should be respected.

4. They welcome the four-power agreement on Berlin and the Soviet–German Treaty.

5. They agree that a conference on security and co-operation could begin after the signature of the Berlin agreement and without undue delay.

6. They believe that the goal of stability and security in Europe would be served by a reciprocal reduction of armed forces and armaments, first of all in Central Europe.

Suggestions for Further Reading

General

BARKER, ELISABETH, *Britain in a Divided Europe 1945–1970*, Weidenfeld and Nicolson, London (1971)

BIRNBAUM, K. E., *Peace in Europe: East–West Relations 1966–1968 and the Prospects for a European Settlement*, Oxford University Press, London (1970)

BUCHAN, ALASTAIR (Ed.), *Europe's Futures, Europe's Choices*, Models of Western Europe in the 1970s: An ISS paperback, Chatto and Windus, London (1969)

DENTON, G. R. (Ed.), *Economic Integration in Europe*, Weidenfeld and Nicolson, London (1969)

DUTOIT, B., *L'Union Sovietique face à l'Integration Européenne*, Lausanne (1964)

KASER, M., *Comecon*, Oxford University Press, London (1967)

KASER, M. and ZIELINSKY, J., *Planning in East Europe*, Bodley Head, London (1970)

LACQUER, M., *Europe Since Hitler*, Weidenfeld and Nicolson, London (1970)

PALMER, M., *Prospects for a European Security Conference*, Political and Economic Planning (P.E.P.): Chatham House, London

P.E.P., *European Unity, Co-operation and Integration*, Allen and Unwin, London (1968)

SAMUELSON, P., *International Economic Relations*, Macmillan, London (1969)

WILES, P. J. D., *Communist International Economics*, Blackwell, Oxford (1968)

WILCZYNSKI, J., *The Economics and Politics of East–West Trade*, Macmillan, London (1969)

Chapter 1
EDEN, SIR A., *Memoirs, Full Circle*, Cassell, London (1960)
FLEMING, D. F., *The Cold War and Its Origins*, Allen and Unwin, London (1961)
HALLE, L. J., *The Cold War as History*, Chatto and Windus, London (1967)
KOHLER, H., *Economic Integration in the Soviet Bloc*, Praeger (1965)
MCNEILL, W. H., *America, Britain, Russia, Survey of International Affairs 1939–1946*, Oxford University Press (1953)
MALLALIEU, W. C., 'The Origins of the Marshall Plan', *Political Science Quarterly* (December 1958)
NORTHEDGE, F. S. and GRIEVE, M. J., *A Hundred Years of International Relations*, Duckworth, London (1971)
SIOTIS, J., 'The Economic Commission for Europe and the Reconstruction of the European System', Carnegie Endowment for International Peace Review: *International Conciliation*, No. 561 (1967)
WHEELER BENNETT, J. W. and NICHOLLS, A., *The Semblance of Peace*, Macmillan, London (1972)
WIGHTMAN, D., *Economic Co-operation in Europe: a Study of the Economic Commission for Europe*, Stevens, London (1956)

Chapter 2
AUSCH, S., *Theory and Practice of CMEA Co-operation,* Akademiai Kiado, Budapest (1972) (in English)
DE LA MAHOTIERE, S., *Towards One Europe*, Penguin (1970)
BROAD, R. and JARRETT, J. R., *Community Europe Today,* Wolff, London (1972)
FELD, W. J., MONTIAS, J. M., PINDER, J., Essays on Aspects of Comecon in: 'The Peoples' Democracies after Prague', College of Europe, Cahiers de Bruges N.S. 25., De Tempel Bruges (1970)
WILCZYNSKI, J., *The Economics of Socialism*, Allen and Unwin (1970)
The 1960 Statutes of Comecon are given in an Appendix to M. Kaser's *Comecon* (see *General*)
The Comecon Comprehensive Programme was published in *Pravda* (7 August 1971) and in '*Neues Deutchland*'. No full, published, English version is known to the author.
The United Nations annual Economic Surveys of Europe from 1965 onwards provide useful information on economic reform in Eastern Europe. There is also a large literature on this subject. The annual General Reports on the Activities of the EEC prepared by the Commission and published in Brussels provide a good survey of the development of the Common Market.

Chapter 3

The book by Dutoit, quoted in the general reading list, contains the full texts of the 17 and 32 Theses.

LE GALL, P., 'L'URSS et l'Unification Européenne', *Revue de Science politique,* **xvii** (February 1967)

LENIN, V. I., *The United States of Europe Slogan* (full English translation in *Collected Works* (English Edition), *Vol.* 21, 339

LUKASZEWSKI, J., 'La CEE et l'Europe de l'Est', *La Revue Nouvelle,* **xlvi** (July–August 1967)

TÖRNUDD, K., *Soviet Attitudes towards Non-Military Regional Co-operation,* Societas Scientiarium Fennica, Helsinki (1963)

ZELLENTIN, G., *Die Kommunisten und die Einigung Europas,* Atheneum Verlag, Frankfurt am Main (1964)

Reference should also be made to the *World Marxist Review* (especially between 1957 and 1960) and to *International Affairs* (Moscow) for articles bearing a Communist discussion of the EEC.

Chapter 4

The annual General Reports on the Activities of the EEC summarise developments in the EEC's external policies.

LOHR, W. Rapport sur les Questions de Politique commerciale commune de la Communante à l'égard des pays à commence d'état, Parlement Européen, Documents de Seance, 1965–1966, No. 10.

ACHENBACH, M. E., Rapport à l'Assemble consultative du Conseil de L'Europe sur l'activité du Parlement Européen du 1er mai 1964 au 30 Avril 1965; Premiere partie: Les relations commerciales entre l'Est et l'Ouest, Parlement Européen, Documents de Seance, 1965–1966, No. 75.

HAHN, K., Rapport sur les problèmes des relations commerciales entre la Communauté et les pays à commerce d'Etat d'Europe orientale, Parlement Européen, Documents de Seance 1967–1968, No. 205

DUTOIT, B., 'Les Relations la Communaute Economique Européenne et le Conseil d'Assistance Economique Mutuelle', *Revue Tiers-Monde,* **ix** (July–December 1968)

IAI (Italian Institute for International Affairs), 'Evoluzione delle Econonomie Orientale e Prospettivi digli Scambi Est-Ovest', Atti de Convegno Internazionale IAI., Milano 21 e 22 Giugno (1968) (contains a section on the commercial policy of the EEC towards Eastern Europe)

PIGASSI, M., Bilan et Perspectives de la Politique Commerciale au sein de la CEE, *Politique Etrangere* (October 1970)

Chapter 5

AIEE, (Association des Instituts d'Etudes européennes), Colloque sur la Communauté Européenne et les Pays de l'Est, Geneva (1969)

KAWAN, L., 'Les Rapports les Communaute's Européennes et les Pays de

l'Est', in: *Les Communautés dans l'Europe*, Université de Bruxelles, Editions de l'Institut de Sociologie (1969)
UN, Economic Bulletins for Europe
EEC(Statistical Office), EEC Foreign Trade Statistics

Chapter 6
United Nations, *Economic Bulletin for Europe*, **22**, No. 1
PROUT, C., *Industrial Co-operation with Eastern Europe*, East European Trade Council (1971)
Carnegie Endowment for International Peace, *International Organisations in Europe and the Changing European System*, second Conference, Geneva (1972) (especially a paper by Dr. Jeno Rédei on Industrial Co-operation between East and West)

Chapters 7 and 8
It is suggested that these speculative chapters can only be judged against the background of wide general reading in the daily and periodical press of the United Kingdom and the other EEC countries and in journals devoted to international affairs.

Index

Index